Blacks and Religion
Volume Two

Blacks and Religion Volume Two

What did Black People contribute to the Origin and Evolution of Judaism, Christianity, Islam, the Indian Religions, and the New Religious Movements?

BY

Robin Walker

REKLAW EDUCATION LTD
London (U.K.)

First published in 2015 by Reklaw Education Limited

ISBN-13: 978-1519746368

ISBN-10: 1519746369

Cover design by Robin Walker

Holy Virgin of Czestochowa, Radomysl Castle, Ukraine, (before 1714 AD).
Photo credit (see below)
Юрий Рудницкий

CONTENTS

OPENING REMARKS

Religion can often be a major source of conflict and controversy between individuals, peoples, nations and races. However, what all the major religions seem to agree upon is their unified efforts to downplay, disregard and remove the role of Black people from their respective histories.

Thus Darren Aronofsky can direct a 2014 film called *Noah* and have an all White cast and even cast a Caucasian to play the role of Ham. A Google search of images of St Augustine, the great Christian theologian, reveals nothing but dishonest iconography fabricated on behalf of the Catholic Church to whiten the great African church Father. Islam teaches that a Black person is important in the history of Islam but, as one website put it: "Bilal was a slave to one of the biggest leaders in Makkah. He was often mistreated because of his colour." In other words, be grateful for just being included and accept whatever low status the story accords you! Similar problems occur with popular presentations of the Buddha and Krishna.

In *Blacks and Religion Volume Two,* I challenge this. I show that Black people are a part of the respectful history of these religions and therefore have as much to do with these religions as anyone else. Therefore Black people who are armed with this information can continue to be movers and shakers in the evolution of religious ideas today and tomorrow just as their ancestors of old. Moreover, this book is a small part of a greater effort to restore Black people to their former position of reverence and respect upon the Earth.

Part One of this book is called *Black Influences in the Origin of Judaism.* It contains a discussion of the origins of the Jews, the origins of certain Jewish religious ideas, and what roles Black people played in influencing those ideas. I discuss documentary evidence, anthropology, archaeology, and genetic evidence to help get to the bottom of Judaism's origins.

Part Two is called *Black Influences in the Origin of Christianity.* It contains a history of the early African church, the origins of certain Christian religious ideas, and what roles Black people played in influencing those ideas. I trace the Christ story, the historical Jesus, the Black Madonna and Child, and Nile Valley influences on these concepts.

Part Three is called *Black Influences in the Origin of Islam and the Indian Religions.* It contains a discussion of the origins of Islam, and the roles Black people played in its inception. There is also a discussion on the origins of Shaivism, Hinduism and Buddhism. What is this discussion doing here? As surprising as it may seem to some, these religions have more to do with Black history than may be apparent at first glance.

Part Four brings the discussion nearer to our modern times and is called *Black Influences in the Origin of the New Religious Movements.* It contains a discussion of the origins of Rastafari, the Moorish Science Temple of America, the Nation of Islam, and Black Liberation Theology. This shows what directions Black theologians of the twentieth century took the discussions of which way forward for Black people. They are role models for where Black theologians of the future could take Black theology.

In putting this book together, I built upon the scholarship of previous writers. I acknowledge my intellectual debts to Professor Yosef ben-Jochannan, whose *African Origins of the Major 'Western' Religions* (US, Black Classic Press, 1970), was a major influence on this book. I would also like to acknowledge the inspiration of Professor John G. Jackson, Professor Charles Finch and Professor Maulana Karenga.

Read and enjoy

Robin Walker 2015

PART ONE

BLACK INFLUENCES IN THE ORIGIN OF JUDAISM

INTRODUCTION

In December 639 CE, Arab armies entered Egypt, conquering from Arabia. A Muslim historian called El-Maqrizi recorded an account of the people they saw on entering that land:

> Know the land of Egypt when the Mussulmans entered it, was full of Christians, but divided among themselves in two sects, both as to race and religion. The one part was made up of men about court and public affairs, all Greek, from among the soldiers of Constantinople ... their views as well as their religion, were for all of them, Melkite; and their number was above three hundred thousand, all Greeks. The other portion was the whole people of Egypt, who were called Qibt, and were of mixed descent; among whom one could not distinguish Copt from Abyssinian, Nubian or Israelite.

This excerpt, quoted from the book *Racial Unity of the Ancient Egyptians and Nubians* by Gert Muller, page 25, is most interesting. In explaining the ethnic diversity of the people that lived in Egypt in the pre-Arab period, the Israelites could not be distinguished from the Nubians or Abyssinians. What does this tell us about the appearance of the early Israelites?

The origin of Judaism is a very vexed and difficult problem to untangle. It is not enough to simply present the facts because all the available facts that are relevant to the discussion are controversial. Scholars of all intellectual persuasions can marshal data to support a myriad of different and conflicting theories. It is not easy to untangle the mess, but I shall attempt to do so in this paper. I shall also clarify what the main issues and controversies are.

Mainstream Judaism teaches that Abraham was the first human to seek out God. On this basis, God chose Abraham and his descendants to become a light unto the nations. Before the time of Abraham, mainstream Judaism teaches that humans worshipped idols and other false deities. If this version of events approximates to the historical truth, then Judaism is of unique and divine origin that cannot be traced to any previous source. This is unlike Christianity, which can be traced back to Judaism, or Islam, which can be traced back to Christianity and Judaism. This raises the question: Is it true that Judaism cannot be traced back to any previous source?

Mainstream Judaism, Christianity, Islam, and Western scholarship in general, all teach that Judaism was the world's first monotheistic religion. How true is this claim? Has this claim helped or hindered the tracing of Judaism to its original sources?

Judaism is also presented as one of the two pillars of 'Western' thought. It is presented as the spiritual and religious pillar. On the other hand, Greek philosophy is presented as the philosophical pillar. In practice, this means that Westerners have a lot riding on the question of Judaic origins. They have built a huge intellectual edifice on this idea. They have a lot invested in it. This raises yet another question: Has this massive intellectual investment been of help or hindrance to tracing Judaism to its original historic sources?

CHAPTER ONE: WHERE SHOULD WE BEGIN THE HISTORY OF THE JEWS?

It is possible that the sacred scrolls of Judaism could be used to trace the origins of Judaism. Christians call this collection of literature the Old Testament. Jews call it the Tanakh. What do the scrolls tell us about how the ancient Jews understood their beginnings? I am of the opinion that the scrolls could be interpreted to show that there are four possible options for where we could begin Jewish history: Adam and Eve in the Garden of Eden, Noah on Mount Ararat, Abraham in Ur, or Moses in Egypt.

Adam and Eve in the Garden of Eden may represent the beginnings of Jewish history. If we could identify where the scroll writers located the Garden and what date they gave it, this may give us a clue to Jewish origins. Most writers, including this author, think that the Garden of Eden was located between the Tigris and the Euphrates Rivers of what is now Iraq. Jewish scholars date the Adam and Eve period to 3760 BCE. This data may indicate that the origin of the Jews is to be found in Mesopotamia dating back to 3760 BCE. Readers should note that a radical and well documented book by Pomegranate Publishing (*Eden: The Biblical Garden Discovered in East Africa,* by Gert Muller, 2013), challenges the mainstream idea that the Garden of Eden was in Iraq. This book locates Eden as the area where Sudan, Ethiopia and Eritrea meet.

Noah and the Ark landing on Mount Ararat may represent new beginnings of Jewish history. Mount Ararat is in the Turkey or Caucasus region. Josephus, the noteworthy Roman Jewish scholar, dated the Flood to 1556 years after the creation of Adam which is 2204 BCE. Other Jewish scholars reckon the Flood was a hundred years later or 2104 BCE. Why the difference? Dr John Jackson, a Church rector, wrote a book called *Chronological Antiquities.* A review of this book appeared in a July 1752 edition of *The Monthly Review or Literary Journal* where we read:

> Another evidence of the corruption of the *Hebrew* copies, is, the disagreement between the western and eastern copies. The western *Hebrew* copies all reckon the flood to commence in the year of the world 1656. But we are told by an author of good credit, that all the *Hebrew* copies of *Genesis* used by the eastern *Jews,* give no more than 1556 years to this period; that is, they place the deluge in the year of the world 1556, and so made the time a century less than the

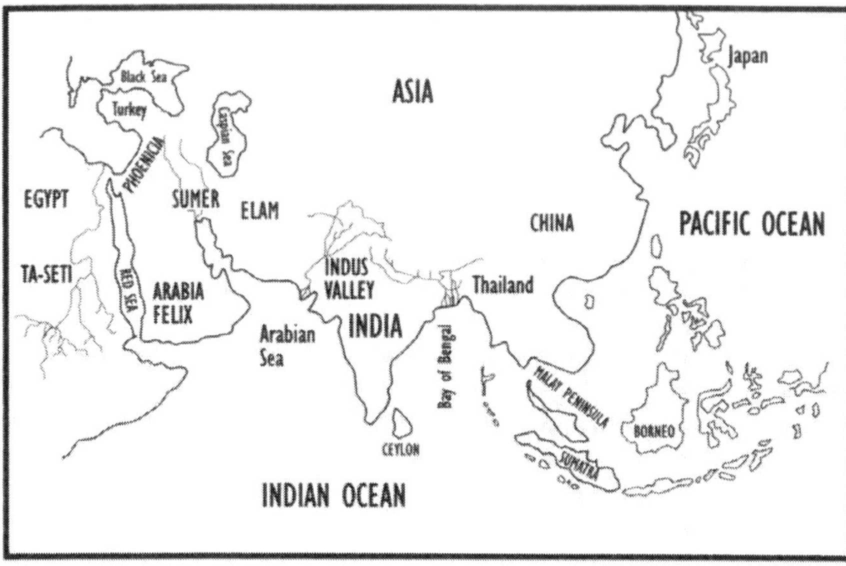

Figure 1. Map of East Africa and Asia. Ta-Seti (later called Kush), Egypt, Phoenicia (also called Canaan), Sumer, and the Indus Valley are important places in the story presented here.

> Western *Jews* did. Hence it appears that the *Babylonian Hebrew* text, which was followed by the eastern *Jews,* left out the century in the age of *Jared* before he begat *Enoch,* which stood in the *Tiberian Hebrew* text, which was used in *Judœa,* and by all the Western *Jews.* The ascribing to *Jared* 62 years instead of 162 before he begat *Enoch,* without any other alteration in the ages of the patriarchs, makes the number of the *Hebrew* chronology from the creation to the Flood 1556, instead of 1656. And so there is no doubt that the alteration was made in the age of *Jared* only, before he begat *Enoch.*

This data may indicate that the origin of the Jews is to be found in the Caucasus dating back to around 2204 or 2104 BCE. For example, Michael Bradley, author of *Chosen People from the Caucasus,* argues that the Jews were originally Caucasians. Readers should note, however, that this conclusion has also been challenged. Pomegranate Publishing's book *Eden: The Biblical Garden Discovered in East Africa,* argues that there is also a Mount Ararat in Ethiopia and make a case why this is even more likely to have been the Biblical setting than the one in the Caucasus.

Abraham in the city of Ur represents the beginnings of the Jewish lineage. Ur was a Sumerian city located in modern Iraq. The Bible makes it clear that the Sumerians were Cushites (Genesis 10: 8-10). I present strong evidence that the Sumerians were largely Black in *When We Ruled,* Chapter 20. Pomegranate Publishing have issued two books on the subject where the evidence is close to definitive--*Black Sumer: The African Origins of Civilisation* and *Black Sumer: The Physical Evidence (Part One* and *Two)*. However, Abraham was descended from the lineage of Shem. He was therefore a Semite. Jewish scholars date his birth to 1948 years from Creation or 1812 BCE. The data may indicate that the Jews were originally a Semitic people living amongst the largely Black people of Sumer.

Moses in Egypt represents the beginning of the development of Jewish law and ritual with the core texts that Judaism uses today. Moses is identified as the author of the first five scrolls of Judaism. This collection of literature is called the Pentateuch by Christians and the Torah by Jews. Rabbinical Judaism teaches that Moses also handed down the Oral Law to the Elders which eventually became the Talmud. Jewish scholars date his birth to 2368 years from Creation or 1392 BCE. This data may indicate that the Jews were originally Ancient Egyptians. I present solid evidence that the Ancient Egyptians were Black Africans in *When We Ruled,* Chapters 4 and 9. Pomegranate Publishing have issued three books on the subject that agree with this position--Anu M'Bantu's *Afro Hair of the Ancient Egyptians and Blackheads, Africans of Mesopotamia,* Gert Muller's *East African and Nubian Origins of the Ancient Egyptians,* and also Gert Muller's *Racial Unity of the Ancient Egyptians and Nubians.*

In my opinion the original Israelites were Semitic Mesopotamians based on the symbolic evidence of Adam and Eve being from Mesopotamia and Abraham being a Semite. Thus of the four examples given above, two of them point to the same Mesopotamian direction. However Pomegranate Publishing does not agree with my conclusions. By locating the Garden of Eden in East Africa, they argue that almost all of my examples given above points to an unambiguous African origin.

However, whilst in Egypt, the Israelites intermarried with the Egyptians. The scrolls claim that a small number of Israelites entered Egypt. However, the scrolls claim that 603,550 able-bodied adult males, not counting Levites, left with Moses during the Exodus 430 years later. We are never told how many wives, non-fighting men, Levites and children also left with Moses. Professor Charles Finch, author of *Echoes of the Old Darkland* places the figure at 2 million people. Based on this figure, it is very likely that significant intermarriage must have been a key to Israelite population growth. The scrolls allude to this. Abraham impregnated an Egyptian slave called Hagar. She was the mother of his child Ishmael (Genesis 16:1-16). Some rabbinical traditions say that Hagar and Keturah, Abraham's second wife mentioned in Genesis 25:1, is actually the same person. If so, then

Hagar could legitimately be presented as Abraham's second wife. Joseph had an Egyptian wife called Asenath (Genesis 41:45). Finally, Moses had a Black wife called Zipporah, daughter of a Midianite chief (Exodus 2:16-21).

In my opinion, when the Israelites left Egypt they could not have been Semitic in racial appearance and would very largely have taken on the racial appearance of the Ancient Egyptians.

CHAPTER TWO: WHAT DO THE CLASSICAL WRITERS SAY ABOUT JEWISH ORIGINS?

The classical writers of ancient Greece and Rome had interesting things to say about Jewish origins. I am indebted to Professor Charles Finch (page 173) whose research forms the basis of this section.

Josephus, the distinguished Roman Jewish scholar, wrote that: "[Ragmus] had two sons, the one of whom, Judadas, settled the Judadeans, a nation of the Western Ethiopians, and left them his name." What does this mean? The term Western Ethiopians meant Black people from Africa and was used in contrast with Eastern Ethiopians which meant Black people from Asia. The term does NOT mean people from the western part of the East African country called Ethiopia! Thus Josephus thought that the people of Judaea were originally Black people from Africa without being specific about which country in Africa they were originally from.

Tacitus, the great Roman historian, wrote: "Many consider them [Jews] to be the progeny of the Aethiopians, who were impelled by fear, and by the hatred manifested against them, to change their settlements in the reign of King Kepheus." Kepheus appears in Greek and Roman literature as a king of Kush. He may well have been a legendary figure and scholars have no idea which Kushite ruler he should be identified with. Nor do we have any idea what dates to assign this legendary figure. Nevertheless, Tacitus is clear that many considered the Jews to originally have been Kushites from Sudan.

Celsus, a second century CE Greek scholar, wrote: "The Jews were a tribe of Egyptians who revolted from the established religion." The Egyptians, even as late as Roman times, were still mostly Black Africans. The Arab occupation and domination of North Africa have not yet happened. Nor was it going to happen until 639 CE. Therefore Celsus, while disagreeing with Tacitus, sees the Jews as being of Egyptian origins rather than of Kushite origins.

Strabo, the great Roman geographer, wrote: "This region [Judaea] lies towards the north; and it is inhabited in general, as in each place in particular, by mixed stocks of people from Aegyptian and Arabian and Phoenician tribes ... But though the inhabitants are mixed up thus, the most prevalent of the accredited reports in regard to the temple at Jerusalem represents the ancestors of the present Judaeans, as they are called, as Aegyptians." Thus at the time that Strabo was writing, the Temple at Jerusalem, the centre of the Jewish religious world, taught that the people of Judaea were originally Egyptians.

In my opinion, the evidence from the classical writers, strong though it is, does not prove that the ancient Israelites were originally Africans TO BEGIN WITH. I believe that in the centuries leading up to the classical period, it was well known that the Jews had come from Africa in relatively recent times, perhaps in some sort of Exodus from Egypt or Kush. Moreover, enough of them still looked like Africans to validate this widespread belief.

Where I disagree with the classical writers is over the issue of ULTIMATE Jewish origins. I believe that the classical writers were unfamiliar with the even earlier traditions that linked the ancient Israelites to Semitic origins and to Mesopotamia BEFORE they entered Africa.

CHAPTER THREE: ARE THERE ANY CLUES FROM THE TANAKH ABOUT ISRAELITE APPEARANCE?

Ra Un Nefer Amen, the leader of the Ausar and Auset society has rightly, in my view, cautioned the Black community from claiming the history and heritage of Judaism as being something that is strictly and solely African. To illustrate his view, he points out the following passage from Ezekiel 16:3, that says: "And say, Thus saith the Lord GOD unto Jerusalem; Thy birth and thy nativity is of the land of Canaan; thy father was an Amorite, and thy mother an Hittite."

The ethnicity of the Canaanites (also called Phoenicians) is a complex question. As I wrote in *When We Ruled,* Chapter 10, the evidence is solid that the prehistoric inhabitants of the region were Negroes. When we get to the historical period, however, the evidence is less clear. The majority of the Phoenician ivories on display in the British Museum clearly show a Negro appearance. With the Amorites and the Hittites, however, these people were almost certainly Caucasians. This may be evidence that the original people of Israel before the Egyptian episode were Semites to begin with, whose numbers were boosted by Caucasians whilst living in Canaan.

Numbers 12:1-11 narrates an interesting story that occurred while the Israelites were living in Egypt:

> And Miriam and Aaron spoke against Moses because of the Cushite woman whom he had married; for he had married a Cushite woman. And they said: 'Hath HaShem indeed spoken only with Moses? hath He not spoken also with us?' And HaShem heard it.-- Now the man Moses was very meek, above all the men that were upon the face of the earth.-- And HaShem spoke suddenly unto Moses, and unto Aaron, and unto Miriam: 'Come out ye three unto the tent of meeting.' And they three came out. And HaShem came down in a pillar of cloud, and stood at the door of the Tent, and called Aaron and Miriam; and they both came forth. And He said: 'Hear now My words: if there be a prophet among you, I HaShem do make Myself known unto him in a vision, I do speak with him in a dream. My servant Moses is not so; he is trusted in all My house; with him do I speak mouth to mouth, even manifestly, and not in dark speeches; and the similitude of HaShem doth he behold; wherefore then were ye not afraid to speak against My servant, against Moses?' And the anger of HaShem was kindled against them; and He departed. And when the cloud was removed from over the Tent, behold, Miriam was leprous, as white as snow; and Aaron

> looked upon Miriam; and, behold, she was leprous. And Aaron said unto Moses: 'Oh my lord, lay not, I pray thee, sin upon us, for that we have done foolishly, and for that we have sinned.

Many people reading this text, especially from a Christian background, will be unfamiliar with the term HaShem. This term is frequently used in Judaism to refer to the deity. It literally means "The Name".

We have already seen that Moses' wife was a Cushite of Black Arab heritage. Moses, Aaron, and Miriam are all siblings. According to the miracle described in verse 10, HaShem turned Miriam White for her sin by speaking negatively against Zipporah. This suggests that Miriam, Moses and Aaron were all non-White to begin with.

The idea of Moses being non-White is given further support by a passage in Exodus Chapter 4:1-9 which reads as follows:

> And Moses answered and said: 'But, behold, they will not believe me, nor hearken unto my voice; for they will say: The lord hath not appeared unto thee.' And HaShem said unto him: 'What is that in thy hand?' And he said: 'A rod.' And He said: 'Cast it on the ground.' And he cast it on the ground, and it became a serpent; and Moses fled from before it. And HaShem said unto Moses: 'Put forth thy hand, and take it by the tail--and he put forth his hand, and laid hold of it, and it became a rod in his hand--that they may believe that HaShem, the G-d of their fathers, the G-d of Abraham, the G-d of Isaac, and the G-d of Jacob, hath appeared unto thee.' And HaShem said furthermore unto him: 'Put now thy hand into thy bosom.' And he put his hand into his bosom; and when he took it out, behold, his hand was leprous, as white as snow. And He said: 'Put thy hand back into thy bosom. --And he put his hand back into his bosom; and when he took it out of his bosom, behold, it was turned again as his other flesh.-- And it shall come to pass, if they will not believe thee, neither hearken to the voice of the first sign, that they will believe the voice of the latter sign.

Thus Moses, according to the story, was able to change his skin colour from whatever-it-was, to white, and back to whatever-it-was. As the African American scholar Professor Joseph Ben Levi pointed out in a lecture, this was one miracle that Europeans never reproduced in the *Ten Commandments* film.

Secondly, this miracle was said to be more impressive, powerful and convincing than being able to turn a staff into a snake. This strongly implies that the skin colour change was dramatic. This would appear to provide support for the notion that Moses himself and his siblings, Miriam and Aaron, were Africans. This also suggests that Miriam's disapproval of Zipporah was not motivated by racial hatred, as is so often believed, but by

Figure 2. Seventeenth century Dutch painting by Jacob Jordaens depicting Moses and Zipporah. While clearly an improvement on the usual depictions, is this really good enough?

ethnic hatred. Miriam and Zipporah were both Black. The disapproval of Moses' choice of wife was because she was neither Jewish, nor Egyptian.

There are other passages in the Tanakh which make reference or analogies to skin colours. The Song of Songs 1:5 says: "I am black, but comely, O ye daughters of Jerusalem, as the tents of Kedar, as the curtains of Solomon." Job 30:30 says: "My skin is black upon me." Jeremiah 14:2 says: "Judah mourneth, and the gates thereof languish; they are black unto the ground." Psalms 119:83 says: "For I am become like a bottle in the smoke." Amos 9:7 says: "Are ye not as children of the Ethiopians unto me, O children of Israel? saith the LORD." There is also another passage that translators have played with. Professor Yosef ben-Jochannan points out that Lamentations 5:10 in some versions is given as "Our skin was black like an oven because of the terrible famine" and has also been rendered as "Our skin is hot as an oven with the burning heat of famine."

The Lamentations reference connects blackness with a famine. Pomegranate Publishing has an interesting explanation of why this might be the case in the book *The Ancient Black Hebrews and Arabs:*

> People of reddish-brown complexion will experience a skin darkening response to trauma, certain illnesses and starvation. This darker colour can be poetically compared to 'coal black'. The medical term for this darkening is called *hyperpigmentation* and is a 'skin sign' of starvation … Hyper-pigmentation tends to be more acute in people with Fitzpatrick skin type 5 and 6 [i.e. skin complexions typical of Beyoncé type 5, or Naomi Campbell type 6].

The *Bible Gateway* website gave the preamble to Psalm 7:1 as "An Ode of David ... which he sang to the LORD concerning the words of Cush, a Benjamite." This raises a question: Who is Cush? The footnote to this passage explains: "The rabbis also maintained that *Cush* was a reference to Saul (cf 1 Sam 9:1)." Saul was the very first of four monarchs of the united kingdoms of Israel and Judah.

Finally, one of the prophetic scrolls was written by a writer known to have been Black. The book of Zephaniah begins 1:1 "The word of the LORD which came unto Zephaniah the son of Cushi, the son of Gedaliah, the son of Amariah, the son of Hizkiah, in the days of Josiah the son of Amon, king of Judah." The name Cushi now has a derogatory meaning amongst modern Israelis. They use it as a strongly negative swearword to mean Black people. Consequently Zephaniah is describing himself as the son of Cushi.

CHAPTER FOUR: IS THERE SURVIVING PHYSICAL EVIDENCE OF THE ANCIENT PEOPLE OF ISRAEL?

The Assyrians were a near White Semitic people who became dominant in around 700 BCE. They left behind important depictions of their near Eastern and African enemies. Among these enemies were the Elamites, Egyptians, Kushites and Judeans. Many scholars have recognised the important scholarly value of this art because it preserves an ethnological picture of the Near East and North-East Africa as it was in the earlier first millennium BCE.

An important English scholar, Sir Harry Johnston examined this art and concluded: "The Elamites of Mesopotamia appear to have been a Negroid people with kinky hair, and to have transmitted this racial type to the Jews and Syrians."

Figure 3. Assyrian depictions of Judeans from the Royal Palace of Ninevah, *c.*700 BCE.

The Reverend C. J. Ball reproduced some of these images in his 1899 text *The Light from the East.* The African-American scholar James Brunson has reproduced them more recently. The Assyrians clearly depicted the Judeans as Negroes.

Professor David Ussishkin of Tel Aviv University presents evidence of a different nature. Valuable archaeological research provided evidence that allowed physical anthropologists to make an assessment of the skulls found at the Judaean city of Lachish:

> The excavation uncovered a mass of human bones, which was estimated by the British to form the remains of fifteen hundred individuals … Remains of 695 skulls were brought to London by the British expedition and were examined there by D. L. Risdon … Curiously, the crania indicate a close racial resemblance to the population of Egypt at that time … Risdon made … the … conclusion … that "the relationships found suggest that the population of the town in 700 B.C.E. was entirely, or almost entirely, of Egyptian origin" … They show, further, that the population of Lachish was probably derived principally from Upper Egypt … If so, this indeed is a conclusion of far-reaching implication.

Pomegranate Publishing present the physical anthropological evidence with much more extensive detail in the book *The Ancient Black Hebrews Vol II: The Forensic Proof Simply Explained* by Gert Muller.

CHAPTER FIVE: CONCLUSIONS ON THE ORIGINS QUESTION

I am of the opinion that the original people that became the Jews were of Semitic Mesopotamian origins. Boosting this population were Caucasian populations of Amorite and Hittite origins, in the land of Canaan. Once the Israelites entered Egypt, they were a small and insignificant people. If the Exodus story has any validity, they must have intermarried greatly with the Egyptians to produce a figure of 2 million people. Some of their greatest leaders had Egyptian or Black Arab wives. When they left Egypt, they were largely a Negro people who were depicted as such in the Assyrian art, and described as such by the Greco-Roman scholars. Some of those historians, however, were unaware of the earlier history in Mesopotamia and Canaan and incorrectly reasoned that the Ancient Israelites were strictly of Egyptian or Sudanese in origin.

The Assyrians and Babylonians attacked the kingdoms of Israel and Judah. These conquests produced two outcomes.

Firstly, some Jews were captured by these conquerors and were brought back to Assyria and Babylonia. These Jews would intermarry with and even assimilate some of their conquerors, Assyrians and Babylonians - both Semitic peoples. These were the Jews that eventually wrote down the traditions handed on from the time of Moses that ultimately became the Tanakh. They also compiled the body of Oral Law that would become the Talmud. We know that the Talmud writers could not have been Black since the Talmud did at one time contain anti-Black passages. Dr John Presley in an interesting paper called *Hebrew Myths and Pseudo Bibliography* quotes one such passage:

> And since you have disabled me from doing ugly things in the blackness of night, Canaan's children shall be born ugly and black! Moreover, because you twisted your head around to see my nakedness, your grandchildren's hair shall be twisted into kinks, And their eyes red; again, because your lips jested at my misfortune, theirs shall swell; and because you neglected my nakedness, they shall go naked, and their male members shall be shamefully elongated. Men of this race are called Negroes; there forefather Canaan commanded them to love theft and fornication, to be banded together in hatred of their masters and never to tell the truth.

Figure 4. Old archival photograph of Jews in Yemen showing rich, dark complexions that contrasts against their light coloured clothing.

David M. Goldenberg, however, insists that a more nuanced position on the Talmud is required. He quotes an eighth century rabbi who wrote this:

> He blessed Noah and his sons -- as it says: "And God blessed them," i.e. with their gifts, and he apportioned the entire earth to them as an inheritance. He blessed Shem and his sons [making them] black and beautiful and he gave them the habitable earth. He blessed Ham and his sons [making them] black as the raven and he gave them the sea coasts. He blessed Japheth and his sons [making] all of them white and he gave them the desert and fields. These are the portions he gave them as an inheritance.

Goldenberg also makes the extraordinary statement: "When we undertake such an objective and thorough investigation, we find a positive perception of Blacks running throughout the rabbinic corpus."

Whichever be the case, the Jews captured by the Assyrians and Babylonians came to dominate the intellectual structure of Judaism in classical and early mediaeval times. Their descendants would have a big impact in southern and western Europe during this period.

Finaly, other Jews (and also Canaanites) fled to other places to avoid the Assyrian and Babylonian onslaughts. Some fled to North Africa to the state of Carthage. Others entered Egypt where they built the famous Temple of Yahu in the city of Elephantine located on the Egypt / Nubia border. Others fled to Yemen and became the Yemeni Jews. Others fled to India and became the Cochin Jews. I speculate that the Falasha Jews of Ethiopia are descended from the Elephantine Jews. As with the Assyrian and Babylonian Jews, these other Jewish populations intermarried with the other nations that they lived amongst.

CHAPTER SIX: DOES THE TANAKH SHOW EVIDENCE OF AFRICAN AND ASIAN INFLUENCE?

It is well known that Jews end their prayers with Amen. Scholars claim that 'Amen' means 'so be it'. However, Amen, also written as Amun, was the chief deity of the ancient Egyptian city of Waset (also known as Thebes). He was also the chief deity of the Kushite city of Jebel Barkal. So when individuals end their prayers with Amen, who are they really praying to?

Many people, especially Christians, believe that Ancient Judaism was the culture to pioneer the practice of circumcising boys. However, the practice of circumcision is known to have taken place in Ancient Egypt and Kush and is, in fact, a general African practice. Professor Cheikh Anta Diop explains this:

> The Egyptians practiced circumcision as early as prehistoric times; they transmitted this practice to the Semitic world in general (Jews and Arabs), especially to those who Herodotus calls Syrians ... Thus, we can understand why the Semites practice circumcision despite the fact that their traditions present no valid justification for it. The weakness of the arguments in Genesis is typical: God asks Abraham (and later Moses) to be circumcised, as a sign of a covenant with Him, without explaining how circumcision, considered from the standpoint of Jewish tradition, can lead to the notion of an allegiance. This is all the more curious because Abraham was allegedly circumcized at the age of ninety ... he married a Negro woman, Hagar, mother of Ishmael, the Biblical ancestor of the second Semitic branch, the Arabs. Ishmael was said to be the historical ancestor of Mohammed. Moses, too, wed a M[i]dianite, and it was in connection with his marriage that the Eternal asked him to be circumcized. What should be noted in these legendary tales is the idea that circumcision was introduced among the Semites only as a result of contact with the Black world ... Only among Blacks does circumcision find an interpretation integrated in a general explanation of the universe, in other words, a cosmogony.

These are not the only connections between Judaism and earlier traditions. A number of stories and passages in the Tanakh have excited the interest of scholars. Among these are the Flood Story, the Birth of Moses, the Ten Commandments, Psalms 104, and Proverbs 22.

The Flood Story and Noah's Ark took on a particular interest when scholars began deciphering the old cuneiform tablets of the Sumerians and

Figure 5. Wall carvings from the Ancient Egyptian Temple of Denderah showing the deity Khnum creating a man on a potter's wheel from clay, assisted by the deity Heket.

the other Mesopotamian peoples. The Sumerians were the original and largely Black inhabitants of Mesopotamia. Flourishing between 3300 and 2609 BCE, the *Epic of Gilgamesh* is their most famous literary creation. Divided into Twelve Tablets, scholars have paid particular attention to the details of the Eleventh Tablet. Albert Champdor, in his book, *Ancient Cities and Temples: Babylon,* gave us the following information:

> On a tablet in Sumerian from Nippur is recorded a story of the Deluge, and another, very similar, is contained in the Epic of Gilgamesh from the Akkadian texts of Assurbanipal's library at Nineveh. In the latter, which is better preserved, a patriarch whose home is at Shurrupak on the Euphrates, Utu-napishtim by name, is warned by the god Ea: 'Tear down this house, build a ship!… Aboard the ship take thou the seed of all living things The ship that thou shalt build Her dimensions shall be to measure. Equal shall be her width and her length …'

The story continues: "And Utu-Napishtim, not without difficulty, built and launched his ship, laden with his family and kin, all living beings, silver and gold; and he battened it down."

> I watched the appearance of the weather
> The weather was awesome to behold ...
> … Consternation over Adad reaches to the heavens,
> Turning to blackness all that had been light
> The (wide) land was shattered like (a pot)!
> For one day the south storm (blew)
> Gathering speed as it blew (submerging the mountains)
> Overtaking the people like a battle.
> No one can see his fellow,
> Nor can the people be recognized from heaven.
> … Six days and (six) nights
> Blows the flood wind, as the south storm sweeps the land
> When the seventh day arrived …
> ... The sea grew quiet, the tempest was still, the flood ceased.
> I looked at the weather; stillness had set in.
> ... And all of mankind have returned to clay.
> The landscape was as level as a flat roof.
> I opened a hatch, and light fell on my face.
> Bowing low, I sat and wept,
> Tears running down my face …
> … On Mount Nisir the ship came to a halt.
> Mount Nisir held the ship fast,
> Allowing no motion …
> … I sent forth and set free a dove.
> The dove went forth, but came back;
> There was no resting-place for it and she turned round.
> … Then I sent forth and set free a raven.
> The raven went forth and, seeing that the waters had diminished,
> He eats, circles, caws, and turns not round.
> Then I let out (all) to the four winds
> And offered a sacrifice ...

Professor Charles Finch, in his book *Echoes of the Old Darkland,* pages 173 and 174, points out that there is an Ancient Egyptian story from the thirteenth century BCE that also has a bearing on this same question. An excerpt reads as follows:

> What is it that hath happened to those who have become like the children of Nut. They have fought fights, they have upheld strifes, they have done evil, they have created hostilities, they have made slaughter, they have caused trouble and oppression. Verily, in all their doings they have made the great to become feeble in all our works. O great THOTH, declare strongly that what TEM hath commanded shall be performed. Thou shalt not seek iniquity, thou shalt not be pained, for their years are nothingness, and their months are drawing to an end, even whilst they are working mischief. [Lord TEM says] I am going to blot out everything I have made. The earth shall enter into the

> watery abyss of NU by means of a raging flood, and will become even as it was in primeval time.

The story of the infant Moses floating down the river Nile in a basket and being discovered by the daughter of the Pharaoh, has its parallels in other stories from Egypt and Mesopotamia. Tsegaye Gabre-Medhin, a one-time Poet Laureate of Ethiopia in *The Origin of the Trinity in Art and Religion* published in *Afrikan Origins of the Major World Religions,* made two comparisons between the Moses story and other traditions: the birth of Horus and the birth of Sargon I.

Plato, a Greek philosopher, recorded a story which he claims is 8000 years old from the Ancient Egyptian city of Saïs. The Egyptian story read as follows:

> Isis feared for the life of her child, Osiris ... Isis made a box from papyrus and reed in which she hid Osiris from the rage of his jealous brother, Set ... At night she closed the lid of the box. She let it float on the Great Nile. The river carried the child far, to the city of Sais, ... as far as the city of Khemisi and farther into Byblos, and as far as the gardens of Melkarth, the King of Bybos, where Isis herself came to nurse Osiris. The transactions of this our city of Saïs, are recorded in our sacred writings during a period of 8000 years.

Plato did not report the information accurately, however. Horus was the correct name of the child of Isis and not Osiris as Plato recorded. The Egyptians believed that Horus was an incarnation of Osiris as well as being his son. Therefore, it is not difficult to see why Plato confused Horus with Osiris.

The Akkadians were a Semitic speaking population that lived just north of the Sumerians. They adopted many aspects of Sumerian culture including the cuneiform script. Sargon I was their most important king. His own chronicle of his life has attractive scholarly attention:

> My city is Azupiranu which lieth on the bank of the Euphrates. My poor mother conceived me. In secret she brought me forth. She set me in a basket of rushes, with bitumen she closed my door. She cast me into the river. The river bore me up unto Aki, the Irrigator ... and the goddess Ishtar came to protect me.

Judaism follows 613 Commandments. However, the Ten Commandments which have also been adopted by the Christians, is of great interest to this discussion.

The Ancient Egyptians had a body of religious literature that scholars call the *Book of the Dead.* Chapter 125 of this book contains a series of sayings that the dead person's soul must be able to truthfully state when being judged in the Hall of the Two Truths in front of Osiris and the 42 judges sitting in judgement. Consequently these sayings represented the conduct of that dead person when they were alive. Dr E. Curtis Alexander reproduced the 42 statements taken from the *Papyrus of Nu* in his book *African Historical Religions: A Conceptual and Ethical Foundation for Western Religions.*

In entering the Hall of the Two Truths, the dead person's soul must address the first judge and state "I have not done iniquity." Addressing the second judge, the dead person must state "I have not done robbe[ry] with violence." Addressing the third church, the dead person must state "I have done violence to no man." Addressing the fourth judge, the dead person must state "I have not committed theft." Addressing the fifth judge, the dead person must state "I have slain neither man or woman." Addressing the sixth judge, the dead person must state "I have not made light the bushel." Addressing the seventh judge, the dead person must state "I have not acted deceitfully." Addressing the eighth judge, the dead person must state "I have not purloined the things which belong unto God." Addressing the ninth judge, the dead person must state "I have not uttered falsehood." In total, there are 42 such sayings that the dead person had to be able to truthfully state that they did not commit when they were alive.

The scroll of Psalms Chapter 104, attributed to King David, has attracted attention. There is an Ancient Egyptian text from the time of Pharaoh Akhenaten called *The Great Hymn to Aten.* Some scholars, including the website Project Augustine, "Faith Seeking Understanding", have demonstrated some remarkable similarities between the two texts indicating that one has evidently been copied from the other:

(Psalms 104) YHWH my God you are very great.
(Hymn to Aten) Sole God beside whom there is none!

(Psalms 104) YHWH, how manifold are your works! In wisdom you have made them all; the earth is full of your creatures.
(Hymn to Aten) How many are your deeds … You made the earth as you wished, you alone, All peoples, herds, and flocks.

(Psalms 104) You make darkness, and it is night, when all the animals of the forest come creeping out.
(Hymn to Aten) When you set in western lightland, Earth is in darkness as if in death

(Psalms 104) The young lions roar for their prey ... when the sun rises, they withdraw, and lie down in their dens.

(Hymn to Aten) Every lion comes from its den

(Psalms 104) When you hide your face, they are dismayed; when you take away their breath, they die
(Hymn to Aten) When you have dawned they live, When you set they die;

(Psalms 104) These all look to you to give them their food in due season.
(Hymn to Aten) You set every man in his place, You supply their needs; Everyone has his food.

(Psalms 104) People go out to their work and to their labor until the evening
(Hymn to Aten) The entire land sets out to work

(Psalms 104) Yonder is the sea, great and wide, creeping things innumerable are there
(Hymn to Aten) The fish in the river dart before you, Your rays are in the midst of the sea.

(Psalms 104) By the streams the birds of the air have their habitation; they sing among the branches
(Hymn to Aten) Birds fly from their nests, Their wings greeting your *ka*

(Psalms 104) You make springs gush forth in the valleys; they flow between the hills ... The trees of YHWH are watered abundantly
(Hymn to Aten) He makes waves on the mountain like the sea, To drench their fields and their towns.

Similarly, the scroll of Proverbs Chapter 22, attributed to King Solomon, has attracted attention. There is an Ancient Egyptian text from the New Kingdom period called *Instructions of Amenemope.* Professor Yosef ben-Jochannan pointed out striking similarities between it and Proverbs 22 that are almost word-for-word. To illustrate ben-Jochannan's ideas, I shall quote from a Wikipedia page entitled *Instruction of Amenemope:*

(Proverbs 22:17-18): "Incline thine ear, and hear the words of the wise, And apply thine heart to my doctrine; For it is pleasant if thou keep them in thy belly, that they may be established together upon thy lips"
(Amenemope, ch. 1): "Give thine ear, and hear what I say, And apply thine heart to apprehend; It is good for thee to place them in thine heart, let them rest in the casket of thy belly; That they may act as a peg upon thy tongue"

(Proverbs 22:22): "Rob not the poor, for he is poor, neither oppress (or crush) the lowly in the gate."
(Amenemope, ch. 2): "Beware of robbing the poor, and oppressing the afflicted."

(Proverbs 22:24-5): "Do not befriend the man of anger, Nor go with a wrathful man, Lest thou learn his ways and take a snare for thy soul."
(Amenemope, ch. 10): "Associate not with a passionate man, Nor approach him for conversation; Leap not to cleave to such an one; That terror carry thee not away."

(Proverbs 22:29): "[if you] You see a man quick in his work, before kings will he stand, before cravens, he will not stand."
(Amenemope, ch. 30): "A scribe who is skillful in his business findeth worthy to be a courtier"

(Proverbs 23:1): "When thou sittest to eat with a ruler, Consider diligently what is before thee; And put a knife to thy throat, If thou be a man given to appetite. Be not desirous of his dainties, for they are breads of falsehood."
(Amenemope, ch. 23): "Eat not bread in the presence of a ruler, And lunge not forward(?) with thy mouth before a governor(?). When thou art replenished with that to which thou has no right, It is only a delight to thy spittle. Look upon the dish that is before thee, And let that (alone) supply thy need."

(Proverbs 23:4-5): "Toil not to become rich, And cease from dishonest gain; For wealth maketh to itself wings, Like an eagle that flieth heavenwards"
(Amenemope, ch. 7): "Toil not after riches; If stolen goods are brought to thee, they remain not over night with thee. They have made themselves wings like geese. And have flown into the heavens."

(Proverbs 14:7): "Speak not in the hearing of a fool, for he will despise the wisdom of thy words"
(Amenemope, ch. 21): "Empty not thine inmost soul to everyone, nor spoil (thereby) thine influence"

(Proverbs 23:10): "Remove not the widows landmark; And enter not into the field of the fatherless."
(Amenemope, ch. 6): "Remove not the landmark from the bounds of the field ... and violate not the widows boundary"

What conclusions can we draw from the similarities? It is clear that Judaism borrowed heavily from the peoples and cultures that they came into contact with. Some of those people were Africans from Africa such as the Ancient Egyptians. Others were Black people in the Middle East such as the Sumerians. It is important to stress however that this does not make the origin of Judaism completely Black. Other influences came from the Amorites, Hittites, Assyrians, and late period Babylonians. All of these peoples left their imprint on Judaism also.

CHAPTER SEVEN: HOW MUCH RELIABLE HISTORY IS THERE IN THE TANAKH?

The Sunday Times Magazine on 16 April 2000 carried a powerful and controversial essay that addressed the historicity of the Tanakh. In one passage, the article admirably summarised the main tenets of the Tanakh story.

> As written from the book of Genesis on, the early biblical story is an epic that underpins the Jewish religion and the nationhood of Israel. Beginning with Earth's creation, it follows the founders of the Jewish people from Noah and the Flood to Abraham, a shepherd who left his home in Mesopotamia and migrated westwards across the desert to Canaan. He was succeeded by his son Isaac, and grandson Jacob--the generations collectively known as the patriarchs. Abraham was already an old man when God promised him the land of Canaan--"All the land which thou seest, to thee will I give it, and to thy seed for ever" (Genesis 13:15)--and told him that his elderly wife, Sarah, would give birth to a son, Isaac. Abraham's faith was tested when God called on him to sacrifice his young child. At the last minute Isaac's life was saved. Isaacs's son Jacob, the smooth man, squabbled with his older brother, Esau, the hairy man, and usurped his father's blessing. Jacob's son Joseph was sold into captivity in Egypt by his jealous brothers. But Joseph prospered. After interpreting Pharaoh's dreams, he rose to high office and was able to welcome his extended family into Egypt at a time of famine in Canaan. But the Israelites were enslaved during their long sojourn in Egypt. Deliverance came through Moses, who as a baby had been hidden in a basket among reeds on the River Nile to avoid slaughter by the Egyptians. Moses was tending sheep when he had a revelation of God in a burning bush, and was told to lead his people back to their Promised Land. The Exodus--the Israelites' escape, the miraculous parting of the Red Sea and their wanderings through the Sinai desert--is a central episode in the Jewish national story, commemorated in the religious festival of Passover. On Mount Sinai, God gave Moses the Ten Commandments. He was succeeded by the more martial Joshua, who invaded Canaan in a blitzkrieg campaign that led to the destruction of Jericho and other cities. The Israelites fanned out in 12 tribes (named after Jacob's sons) across the hill country of Canaan, where their control was consolidated under charismatic leaders, known as judges. Harassed by the Philistines from the coast, they united for a period of kingship under Saul and then Bethlehem-born David, who had defeated the Philistine champion, Goliath. David made Jerusalem the capital of his united monarchy. His son Solomon strengthened this rule, building a great temple in Jerusalem and fortifying far flung cities, including Megiddo, Hazor and Gezer. Or so the Old Testament records. Under Solomon's son Rehoboam the

> monarchy split, with Israel going its own way in the north and Judah in the south. This fatal division was exploited by their neighbours: Israel was destroyed by the Assyrians around 722BC. Judah was conquered by the Babylonian king Nebuchadnezzar in 586BC and its leaders forced into exile in Babylon.

The article eventually dropped a series of bombshells on this story:

> All the more unusual then that, in November, Ze'ev Herzog, a professor of archaeology at Tel Aviv University, broke ranks and, in an article for the Israeli newspaper Ha-aretz, suggested that biblical archaeology was a spent force and that--as history, at least--the Old Testament was bunk.

'Bunk' seems to be an unusually strong word to use. The article continues with further information that might justify the use of such a strong word:

> After a century of extensive excavations in Israel, he wrote, archaeologists could report that "the Israelites were never in Egypt, did not wander in the desert, did not conquer the land in a military campaign and did not pass it on to the 12 tribes of Israel. Perhaps even harder to swallow is that the united monarchy of David and Solomon, which is described by the Bible as a regional power, was at most a small tribal kingdom". To fuel the fire, he added that "It will come as an unpleasant shock to many" that the God of Israel, YHWH [Yahweh or Jehovah], had a female consort and that the early Jews only adopted monotheism around the 7th century BC and not at Mount Sinai around 1250. All hell broke loose, not just because of what he said, but for the manner and timing. Herzog was accused of breaking the archaeologists' code by revealing a closed academic debate to the public.

Many readers reading this passage for the first time may be surprised that there is such a thing as an archaeologists' code. Moreover many will find this surprising that the chief argument against Professor Herzog was that he should not have revealed this debate to the public. This strongly suggests that many archaeologists are already in agreement with the actual basis of his position. Their chief concern seems to have been making sure that the general public never becomes aware of this information.

The information has, however, had an impact on Judaism. An article appeared on the Internet in 2002 called *As Rabbis Face Facts, Bible Tales are Wilting* by Michael Massing. The article describes the actions taken by the United Synagogue of Conservative Judaism in the light of the new archaeological data.

> Abraham, the Jewish patriarch, probably never existed. Nor did Moses. The entire Exodus story as recounted in the Bible probably never occurred. The

same is true of the tumbling of the walls of Jericho. And David, far from being the fearless king who built Jerusalem into a mighty capital, was more likely a provincial leader whose reputation was later magnified to provide a rallying point for a fledgling nation. Such startling propositions--the product of findings by archaeologists digging in Israel and its environs over the last 25 years--have gained wide acceptance among non-Orthodox rabbis. But there has been no attempt to disseminate these ideas or to discuss them with the laity--until now. The United Synagogue of Conservative Judaism, which represents the 1.5 million Conservative Jews in the United States, has just issued a new Torah and commentary, the first for Conservatives in more than 60 years. Called "Etz Hayim" ("Tree of Life" in Hebrew), it offers an interpretation that incorporates the latest findings from archaeology, philology, anthropology and the study of ancient cultures. To the editors who worked on the book, it represents one of the boldest efforts ever to introduce into the religious mainstream a view of the Bible as a human rather than divine document. "When I grew up in Brooklyn, congregants were not sophisticated about anything," said Rabbi Harold Kushner, the author of "When Bad Things Happen to Good People" and a co-editor of the new book. "Today, they are very sophisticated and well read about psychology, literature and history, but they are locked in a childish version of the Bible."

CHAPTER EIGHT: DID CAUCASIAN JEWS FROM EASTERN EUROPE HIJACK A BLACK AND BROWN RELIGION?

With the publication of Arthur Koestler's book, *The Thirteenth Tribe,* published in 1976, scholars outside the mainstream but increasingly including geneticists in the mainstream have pursued very controversial questions. The most acrimonious of these were whether or not Eastern European Jews could be traced back to the ancient peoples of Israel and Judah. Koestler's suggested that Eastern European Jews were in fact descended from eighth century CE converts from Turkey and Southern Russia with no links to Ancient Judaism.

Koestler's research concerns the rise and fall of the Khazar Empire which flourished in southern Russia and Turkey in mediaeval times. What we know about the Khazars comes from two key mediaeval sources--a detailed letter and a geography book.

The oldest of these two sources dates from around 950 CE. It was a detailed letter written by a Khazarian ruler to a Jewish scholar living in Spain called Hasdai Ibn Shaprut. Apparently Hasdai began the correspondence by sending word to the Khazarian ruler to clarify facts about the Khazar Empire. Hasdai wanted to know about their lineage. He also wanted to know how come they were practising Judaism. King Joseph of the Khazars gave detailed answers to Hasdai Ibn Shaprut.

The second key source was *The Book of the Roads and Kingdoms.* Dating from 1067 CE, this was a geography book written by Al Bakri, a Muslim geographer living in the Spanish city of Cordova.

These sources tell us that the Khazars of Turkey and southern Russia wanted to acquire a modern religion but wanted to remain ideologically independent of the Byzantine Empire that professed Christianity and the Islamic Empire. In weighing up the three Abrahamic religions, they chose Judaism to retain their spiritual independence from the two other powers. However, small numbers of Jews from older lineages fleeing Byzantine repression migrated to Khazaria and became religious leaders and teachers of the Khazars.

King Joseph's letter gave a number of key facts. He reports the belief that the Khazarian people consider themselves descended from Togarmah in the scroll of Genesis. Togarmah was, incidentally, of the lineage of Japeth, one of the three sons of Noah. Togarmah was not of the lineage of Shem. Therefore, the Khazars did not consider themselves to be Semites. Incidentally, Genesis 10:2-3 says: "The sons of Japheth: Gomer, and Magog, and Madai, and Javan, and Tubal, and Meshech, and Tiras. And the sons of Gomer: Ashkenaz, and Riphath, and Togarmah."

King Joseph narrates that Bulan was the first king of Khazaria to choose Judaism in around 740 CE. During the time of a later king, Obadiah, Judaism became the state religion with mass conversions of its people. The Obadiah period is around 800 CE.

According to Arthur Koestler, the people of the Khazar Empire eventually adopted the Hebrew script which they used to write their own language. The Khazarian language was originally related to Turkish. However, in the thirteenth century, the Mongols invaded Khazaria and destroyed it. A huge proportion of the Khazar people fled to Poland where the elite of that country were German speakers. In time, the descendants of the Khazarians living in Poland would fuse their language with that of the German speakers of Poland. As before, they wrote this new synthesised language with the Hebrew script. According to Arthur Koestler, this is the origin of Yiddish. These Eastern European Jews would become known as Ashkenazi Jews. They represent the overwhelming majority of modern Judaism.

Does this mean that Caucasian Jews have hijacked Judaism? There are three problems with this scenario. Firstly it assumes that there is such a thing as the Jewish race. This is a controversial question but it is probably true to say that Judaism represents a religion rather than a race. It is therefore incorrect to say that any group of people have hijacked the religion.

Secondly, nearly all Sephardic Jews today are Caucasians. Similarly a large proportion of the Mizrahi Jews are, if not Caucasians, much closer to Caucasians than they are to any other major racial group.

Thirdly, the genetic research does not support such a conclusion. Mainstream and impeccable sources have concentrated their efforts on what is popularly called the Cohen Gene. These are genetic markers which show a distinction between the priestly class of Jews and the masses of ordinary people. Since membership of the priestly class is hereditary and supposedly represents descent from Aaron, some geneticists argue that there really is such a thing as a Jewish race, and these genetic markers offer proof. More detailed information on this is on the Wikipedia page *Y-chromosomal Aaron.*

Why is this significant? Genetic research conducted into the Ashkenazi Jews show that the priestly class have the same genetic markers and distinctions between themselves and the masses of ordinary Ashkenazi people. If Arthur Koestler is correct, these genetic markers should not actually exist. How do we explain this? It is always possible that the priestly class of the Ashkenazi have the genetic marker because they were descended from Byzantine Jews whose lineages may well be ancient. It could also be that Koestler research was in error. I do not know which is the correct position.

The genetic research, however, threw up yet another surprise. Father da Silvera, a Portuguese Jesuit, in describing his visit to the mediaeval Empire of Munhumutapa in southern Africa mentions the presence of Jews in that empire. The descendants of that population, called the Lemba, have become of great interest to geneticists.

The Lemba, like other Jews, have a social distinction between the masses of ordinary people and the elites. The surprising genetic fact is the elites show as strong a concentration of the Cohen genetic marker as any Caucasian Jewish people. The New York Times explained this in a 1999 article called *DNA Backs a Tribe's Tradition of Early Descent from the Jews,* from which I cite the following extracts:

> Dr. Hammer, Dr. Skorecki and their colleagues reported in 1997 that they had analyzed the Y chromosomes of priests and lay Jews. They found that a particular pattern of DNA changes was much more common among the priests than among laymen. The pattern was equally recognizable in Ashkenazic and Sephardic priests, even though these two branches of the Jewish population have long been geographically separated. A colleague in Dr. Hammer's and Dr. Skorecki's research was Neil Bradman, a businessman who is now chairman of the Center for Genetic Anthropology at University College, London ... One recruit to Mr. Bradman's project is David B. Goldstein, a population geneticist at Oxford University in England. Dr. Goldstein set about refining Dr. Hammer's work so as to develop a better genetic signature of Jewish populations ... He found a particular set of genetic mutations at these nine sites that was strongly associated with the priestly caste, not so common among lay Jews, and very rare in non-Jewish populations. Unlike forensic DNA markers, which are chosen to be almost wholly specific to individuals, this cohen-associated genetic signature cannot be used to say who is or who is not a priest. But it is highly diagnostic of whether a population has Jewish ancestry, Dr. Goldstein said. He finds that 45 percent of Ashkenazi priests and 56 percent of Sephardic priests have the cohen genetic signature, while in Jewish populations in general the frequency is 3 to 5 percent ... As part of Mr. Bradman's project on the relationship of Jewish populations, he then tested DNA samples collected from the Lemba. And last month, at a conference on human evolution

held at the Cold Spring Harbor Laboratory in Long Island, Dr. Goldstein reported that 9 percent of Lemba men carried the cohen genetic signature, and of those who said they belonged to the Buba [i.e. elite] clan, 53 percent had the distinctive sequences. These proportions are similar to those found among the major Jewish populations.

CONCLUSIONS

The pages presented here so far show that it is difficult to write a coherent history of the followers of Judaism because every chapter is controversial. Thus I will present my opinions which I believe represents the simplest reading of the available evidence.

The people who would become Jews were originally Semitic Mesopotamians. They may have dated back to Sumerian times. Whilst they lived amongst the Sumerians, they were a Semitic and not a Black people. These are the people represented in the Biblical scrolls by Abraham and his family.

This burgeoning population migrated westwards to Canaan. The prehistoric Canaanites, known as the Natufians, were certainly Black. However, moving from prehistoric to historic times, the ethnic picture is much less straightforward. Despite this lack of certainty, the Nimrud ivories depict the majority of the Phoenicians, as the Canaanites were later called, as Negroes. However, the people that would later be known as Jews in the land of Canaan intermarried with Caucasian populations such as the Amorites and Hittites.

At some point in the story, the Jews entered Egypt. The Biblical scrolls tell the story of how they entered Egypt and were later led out by Moses. While in Egypt the Israelites intermarried heavily with the ancient Egyptians over a 430 year period where they were culturally, linguistically, and racially absorbed by the Egyptian population. Thus, by the time of Moses, the Jews were largely Negroes.

However, the Ancient Egyptian historian Manetho (as quoted by Josephus) recorded a very different story. He tells of how the Jews entered Egypt as part of a conquering group called the Hyksos. These conquerors ruled Egypt as the Fifteenth and Sixteenth Dynasties. After the Sixteenth Dynasty was chased out of Egypt by the indigenous Seventeenth and Eighteenth Dynasty rulers, the Hyksos founded the city of Jerusalem. It is possible that the chasing out of the Hyksos is the same story that was spun in the Biblical scrolls as the Exodus.

It should be fairly obvious, that the Biblical story of the Jews being slaves in Egypt and the story of the Jews being conquerors of Egypt, as told by Manetho, cannot be harmonised with each other. Moreover, there is an additional argument put forward by some scholars who claim that Moses was a real person, mentioned by different classical authors. However, there is no evidence that he was a Jew. Some claim he was actually an indigenous Egyptian priest whose teachings have been hijacked by Judaism. Again, this idea cannot be harmonised with the other ideas presented. For the record, I have no idea which version of events is the correct one.

Then we have the famous stele associated with Nineteenth Dynasty Egyptian Pharaoh Merneptah. Like all Egyptian rulers, his dates are disputed, but I give them as 1328 to 1308 BCE. Other scholars (incorrectly) date him a century later. Which ever be the case, Wikipedia present the relevant part of the inscription as:

> The princes are prostrate, saying, "Peace!"
> Not one is raising his head among the Nine Bows.
> Now that Tehenu (Libya) has come to ruin,
> Hatti is pacified;
> The Canaan has been plundered into every sort of woe:
> Ashkelon has been overcome;
> Gezer has been captured;
> Yano'am is made non-existent.
> Israel is laid waste and his seed is not;
> Hurru is become a widow because of Egypt.

Notice that the second to last line of the excerpt mentions Israel. This suggests that in the fourteenth century BCE, Israel existed as a state within the Canaan region. What do we make of this?

One plausible story could be this. The Israelites were indeed the Hyksos who ruled in Egypt as the Fifteenth and Sixteenth Dynasties (2545-1709 BCE). Indigenous rulers of the Seventeenth and Eighteenth Dynasty broke their power and chased most of them out in 1709 BCE where they fled to Palestine and established a state. This same kingdom was the one "laid waste" by Pharaoh Merneptah (1328 to 1308 BCE) in the raid described in the stele. What is the problem with this interpretation?

Scholars would have a problem with this version of events because (i) it contradicts the Tanakh narrative of the Israelites being enslaved in Egypt, and (ii) it implies that a state existed in Israel before 1308 BCE. Even "short" chronologists would place the end of Merneptah's reign at 1203 BCE. The problem with this is that the Tanakh places the start of the reign of Saul, the first king of Israel and Judah, around 1050 BCE, i.e. much later.

Thus the Merneptah stele alludes to a pre-history of Israel that is NOT RECOGNISED by the Tanakh. On the other hand, the time period from King Saul to King Solomon (1050 to 931 BCE), the period RECOGNISED AND VALORISED by the Tanakh, has left behind very little archaeological evidence. This is why some scholars question the historical validity of the Tanakh.

At some point in the story, and CONTRARY to Professor Ze'ev Herzog, there IS archaeological evidence that the Jews left Egypt for Palestine. This evidence is NOT the same evidence as the Exodus, since THIS evidence is much later than the alleged period of the Exodus. The archaeologists claim that the Jews built the city of Lachish. The skulls from Lachish, as analysed by D. L. Risdon, suggest that these Jews were originally Upper Egyptians. The Assyrians attacked these same people, and the Nineveh palace wall carvings clearly show that these Jews (of Lachish) were Negroes. I believe that Professor Ze'ev Herzog was, understandably, reluctant to deal with this evidence.

The archaeology of early Israel and its history is, as Professor Ze'ev Herzog point out, controversial indeed. This has led many to deny the existence of Abraham, Moses, Aaron, et cetera. What is not controversial, however, is that archaeologists have found a synagogue on Elephantine Island (Temple of Yahu) together with a cache of sixth and fifth century BCE manuscripts, on the Egyptian and Nubian border.

Professor A. H. Sayce wrote about this in 1911. On page 104 of his article, we read the following:

> A discovery, indeed, which I have made in the sandstone quarries east of Assuan proves that the temple was on as large a scale as the leading Egyptian ones and that it was built much in the same style. One of the quarries there has been "earmarked" in five different places for the exclusive use of the Jewish temple, the abbreviated word ... which is employed in the papyri to denote "house" or "temple" ... being engraved on the rocks that marked its boundaries. The letters are ligatured as in the papyri, and they have precisely the same forms. In more than one place the base of a column, or rather of the drum of a column, has been left in the native rock, and we can therefore ascertain what the size of each column was. The three I have found all alike measure 85 centimetres in diameter or nearly 3 feet, and will therefore bear comparison with the columns of the great Egyptian sanctuaries. It would seem that granite as well as sandstone was employed; at all events the base of a smaller column of granite is lying at the foot of the quarry, where I also came across some fragments of Jewish pottery. It is clear, therefore, that at the time the Temple was erected, the Jews were not only a large and wealthy community at Elephantine but also that they must have possessed great political influence. It

> is not wonderful that the priests of Khnum looked with jealous eyes upon them and their rival shrine and seized the first opportunity of bringing about its destruction.

This strongly suggests that Jews of Egypt and Kush certainly existed and unlike the Israel examples contested by Ze'ev Herzog remains uncontroversial and uncontested. Even Professor Simon Schama affirms the Elephantine data in his well-respected television documentary series *The Story of the Jews.*

Then we have the controversial genetic evidence. If Moses did not exist, as some claim, then presumably Aaron, his brother, did not exist either. The Cohen genetic marker is based on the idea that the priestly class of the Jews are descended from Aaron. How can we explain this genetic evidence, if Aaron didn't exist? Are the geneticists making this all up to provide evidence for Aaron? If the geneticists are making this all up, why have they included the Lemba of South Africa in their research? Surely it would have been much simpler to just leave them out. Having included the Lemba, the geneticists claim that they have as high a concentration of the Cohen genetic marker as White Jews. How does this affect the writing of Jewish history? There are no easy answers to these questions.

The classical writers of southern Europe state traditions linking the Jews to Egyptian or Kushite origins. This strongly suggests that the Jews of classical times were much darker and much more Negroid than is generally the case today. This also suggests that there must have been considerable intermarriage between the Jews of the Middle East, North Africa, and southern Europe with non-Black peoples of these regions that took place after the Babylonian captivity. This considerably lightened the complexions of the Jewish populations of these regions over many generations. This is what must have happened to the Mizrahi and the Sephardi Jews.

While the role and importance of the Khazar Empire is disputed by many scholars. It is undeniable that many Eastern European Jews are descended from this empire. Since the founders of this empire did not consider themselves to be Semites, the use of the term anti-Semitism by peoples descended from the Khazar Empire, to describe hatred against them or even to silence criticism against them is not an appropriate or an accurate terminology. Whether this population were converts to Judaism or an ancient lineage perhaps descended from Jews that moved north after the Babylonian captivity will remain a vexed question.

Figure 6. Professor Rabbi Taamrat Emmanuel (*c.*1888-1963) was the most internationally prominent figure in the Falasha or Beta Israel community in Ethiopia in the 1930s.

There are many questions about the history of Judaism in Africa. I speculate that the Falasha Jews of Ethiopia are descended from the Elephantine Island Jews. Until quite recently, some scholars considered their form of Judaism to be older and more authentic than other forms of Judaism. Significantly, their Judaism does not include the Talmud. However, no scholarship claims that the Falasha Jews of Ethiopia carry the Cohen genetic marker. Is this evidence that the Falashas are converts? Conversely, is this evidence that the genetic marker evidence is a fraud? I cannot give satisfactory answers to these questions.

Jewish populations are also known to have existed in the ancient West Africa. Dr Runoko Rashidi found an eleventh century source that told of an ethnic group called the Bafour that lived in the Empire of Ancient Ghana. The source says that before the dominance of Islam, the Bafour were Blacks professing Judaism. The famous Timbuktu Chronicle called *Tarikh Al Fattash,* compiled in the sixteenth and seventeenth centuries, gave details of a Jewish population living within the Songhai Empire. Professor Christopher Wise edited and published this chronicle. What happened to these Jewish populations? Finally, the Igbo and British scholar, Olaudah Equiano, writing in the eighteenth century stated that his people, the Igbos (of Nigeria), are related to Jews. Some authorities are taking these Igbo claims seriously.

BIBLIOGRAPHY

E. Curtis Alexander, *African Historical Religions: A Conceptual and Ethical Foundation for Western Religions,* US, ECA Associates, 1984, pp.19-21

Yosef ben-Jochannan, *The Myth of Genesis and Exodus,* US, Black Classic Press, 1974, pp.50, 65-66

Bible Gateway, *Psalm 7:1,* see https://www.biblegateway.com/passage/?search=Psalm+7%3A1&version=AMP

Michael Bradley, *Chosen People from the Caucasus,* US, Third World Press, 1992. pp.115-155

Albert Champdor, *Ancient Cities and Temples: Babylon,* UK, Elek Books, 1958, pp.12-13

Cheikh Anta Diop, *The African Origin of Civilization: Myth or Reality?* US, Lawrence Hill Books, 1974, pp.135-136

Olaudah Equiano, *The Life of Olaudah Equiano or Gustavus Vassa, the African,* US, Dover, 1999, pp.17-22

Charles Finch, *Echoes of the Old Darkland,* US, Khenti, 1991, pp.139, 173-174

Tsegaye Gabre-Medhin, *The Origin of the Trinity in Art and Religion,* in *Afrikan Origin of the Major World Religions,* edited by Amon Saba Saakana, UK, Karnak House, 1991, p.104

David M. Goldenberg, *The Curse of Ham: A Case of Rabbinic Racism?* see http://www.academia.edu/2915219/The_Curse_of_Ham_A_Case_of_Rabbinic_Racism

Hemel Hermstein, *Black Sumer: The African Origins of Civilisation,* UK, Pomegranate Publishing, 2012

Hemel Hermstein, *Black Sumer: The Physical Evidence* (Part One), UK, Pomegranate Publishing, 2013

Hemel Hermstein, *Black Sumer: The Physical Evidence* (Part Two), UK, Pomegranate Publishing, 2013

Review of John Jackson, *Chronological Antiquities,* in *The Monthly Review or Literary Journal, Volume 7,* edited by Ralph Griffiths, George Edward Griffiths, July 1752, p.6

Sir Harry Johnston is quoted in *Man, God and Civilization,* by John G. Jackson, US, Citadel Press, 1972, p.243

Tamar Kadari, *Hagar: Midrash and Aggadah,* in *Jewish Women's Archive: Encyclopaedia,* see http://jwa.org/encyclopedia/article/hagar-midrash-and-aggadah

Arthur Koestler, *The Thirteenth Tribe,* UK, Pan Books, 1976

Michael Massing, *As Rabbis Face Facts, Bible Tales Are Wilting,* 2002, see http://www.freerepublic.com/focus/news/643380/posts

Anu M'Bantu, *Afro Hair of the Ancient Egyptians and Blackheads, Africans of Mesopotamia,* UK, Pomegranate Publishing, 2013, pp.7-48

Anu M'Bantu and Gert Muller, *The Ancient Black Hebrews and Arabs,* UK, Pomegranate Publishing, 2013, p.29

Gert Muller, *East African and Nubian Origins of the Ancient Egyptians,* UK, Pomegranate Publishing, 2013

Gert Muller, *Eden: The Biblical Garden Discovered in East Africa,* UK, Pomegranate Publishing, 2013, pp.170-172, 177-182

Gert Muller, *Racial Unity of the Ancient Egyptians and Nubians,* UK, Pomegranate Publishing, 2013, pp.7-17, 25, 29-99

Gert Muller, *The Ancient Black Hebrews Vol II: The Forensic Proof Simply Explained,* UK, Pomegranate Publishing, 2014, pp.13-86

John Presley, *Hebrew Myths and Pseudo Bibliography,* in *GRAVESIANA The Journal of the Robert Graves Society,* Volume I, Number II, December 1996, pp.170-171

Project Augustine, "Faith Seeking Understanding", *Parallelism between "The Hymn to Aten" and Psalm 104,* see http://projectaugustine.com/biblical-studies/ancient-near-east-studies/parallelism-between-the-hymn-to-aten-and-psalm-104/

Runoko Rashidi, *Black Star: The African Presence in Early Europe,* US, Books of Africa, 2011, pp.80-81

A. H. Sayce, *The Jewish Garrison and Temple in Elephantine,* in *Expositor,* August 1911, pp.97-116

Simon Schama (presenter), *The Story of the Jews: Part One,* UK, BBC Television, 2013

David Ussishkin, *The Conquest of Lachish by Sennacherib,* Israel, Tel Aviv University Publications of the Institute of Archaeology (Number 6), 1982, pp.56-57

Nicholas Wade, *DNA Backs a Tribe's Tradition of Early Descent from the Jews,* in *New York Times,* 9 May 1999, see http://www.nytimes.com/1999/05/09/us/dna-backs-a-tribe-s-tradition-of-early-descent-from-the-jews.html?pagewanted=all

Robin Walker, *When We Ruled: Second Edition,* UK, Reklaw Education, 2013, pp.117-132, 317-345, 348-352, 685-694

Wikipedia, *Instruction of Amenemope,* see https://en.wikipedia.org/wiki/Instruction_of_Amenemope

Wikipedia, *Merneptah Stele,* see https://en.wikipedia.org/wiki/Merneptah_Stele

Wikipedia, *Y-chromosomal Aaron,* see https://en.wikipedia.org/wiki/Y-chromosomal_Aaron

Christopher Wise ed., *Ta'rikh al fattash: The Timbuktu Chronicles 1493-1599,* US, Africa World Press, 2011, pp.120-121

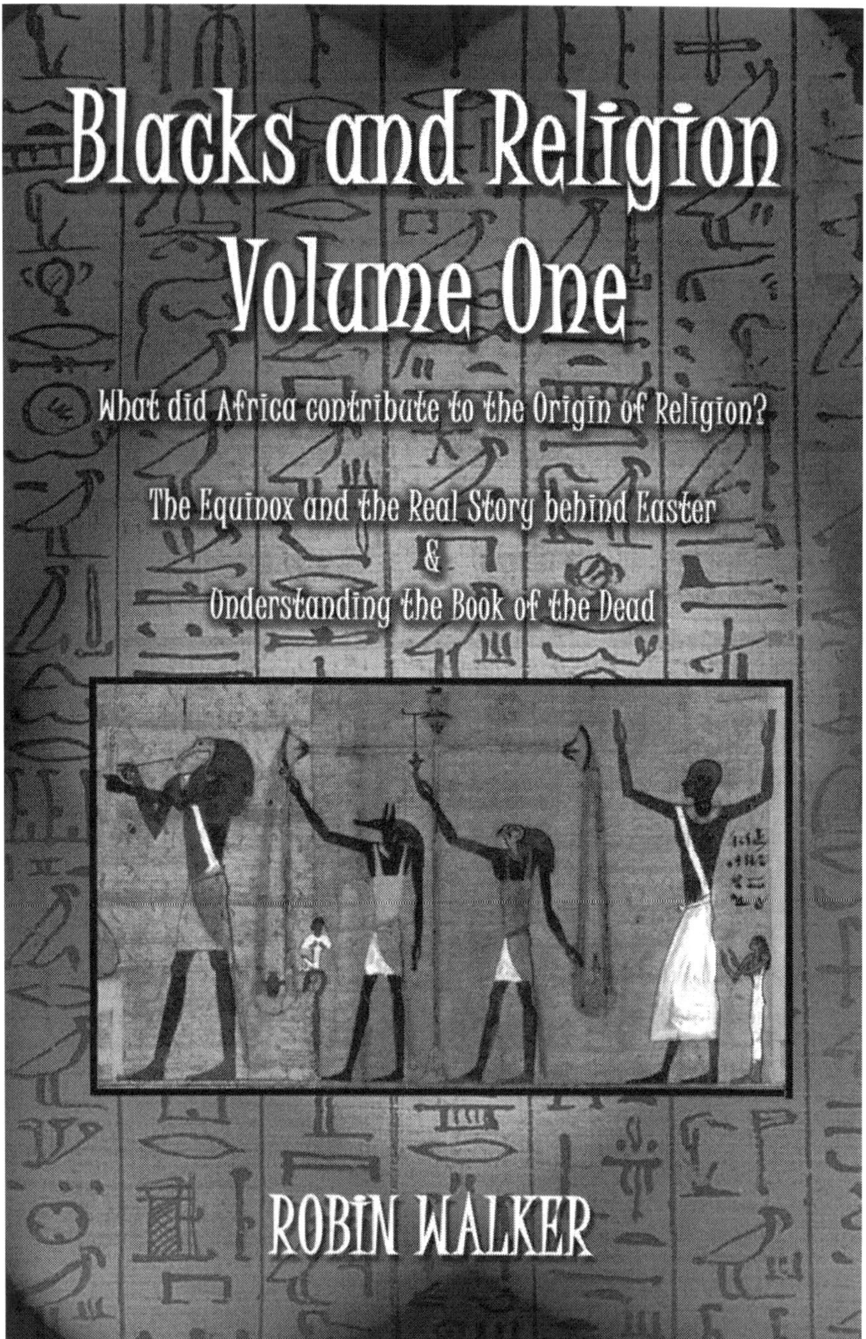

Also available in this series

PART TWO

BLACK INFLUENCES IN THE ORIGIN OF CHRISTIANITY

INTRODUCTION

Many years ago I came across a two-volume book of great scholarly importance. Professor Yosef ben-Jochannan and Professor John G. Jackson frequently referenced the book and both spoke highly of it. Written by Godfrey Higgins in 1836, the book had a strange but imposing title *ANACALYPSIS,* which is a rare word and apparently means "I have discovered it". The subtitle to this book was *an attempt to draw aside the veil of the Saïtic Isis.*

Who was the Saïtic Isis? Dr Runoko Rashidi tells us that the Ancient Egyptians worshipped a goddess called Neith. This deity is not Isis, but shared some similarities with her. The centre of Neith worship was in the Ancient Egyptian city of Saïs. This goddess was typically veiled and there is an inscription from the House of Neith which read: "I am whatever was, or is, or will be; and my veil no mortal has ever took up." This suggests that underneath the veil of Neith is a secret that no mortal has ever seen. Godfrey Higgins believes his book draws aside the veil and thus reveals the secret. This is a very bold claim indeed!

St Augustine was a fourth century theologian. He was from North Africa, and was considered the greatest Father of the Christian church. He is known for writing the *Confessions* and the *City of God.* Mr J. A. Rogers, the great Jamaican historian, quoted an interesting passage from a little-known text called *Retract,* where Augustine said: "What is now called the Christian religion has existed among the ancients and was not absent from the beginning of the human race until Christ came in the flesh from which time the true religion which existed already began to be called Christian."

What was Christianity? Christianity was a religion that attempted to bring Judaism to the non-Jewish masses. By the time Christianity was born, Judaism had already agreed which scrolls constituted the basic tenets of Judaism. The scrolls were collectively known as the Tanakh. When Jesus came on the scene, new manuscripts were written about him and his followers. Four main Gospels were written about Jesus. No one is entirely sure who wrote these documents, but tradition ascribes them to Matthew, Mark, Luke and John. Another Gospel, attributed to Barnabas, is favoured by the Muslims. There are hundreds of other Gospels that did not make it into what was going to evolve into the New Testament. Among these were the Gospel of Mary, Protevangelion, Gospel of the Infancy of Jesus Christ, Gospel of Mary Magdalene, Gospel of the Egyptians, et cetera. In time, the Church would bring together the Tanakh scrolls, which would collectively be known in Christianity, as the Old Testament, and the new texts, which would collectively be known as the New Testament. In addition, Christian theologians would give new and fresh interpretations to the Old Testament texts as these were absorbed into Christianity.

CHAPTER ONE: THE STORY OF THE AFRICAN CHURCH

There was an early church history in North Africa. Professor J. C. deGraft-Johnson, the Ghanaian author of the superb *African Glory,* did much to document that early history. What follows here is largely based on his research.

At the time of the early church history, most of North Africa was ruled by the Roman Empire. The Romans controlled Carthage, Numidia and Egypt. They also ruled much of Europe and Asia Minor. They did not, however, rule in Kush or Ethiopia. It must be remembered that this period of history is well before the Arabian rule of North Africa, consequently the North Africans were still indigenous Black Africans.

The Roman Empire was undergoing a number of political and economic problems. Rising price inflation caused misery for the peasants and lower classes. The authorities found it increasingly difficult to collect taxes due to high prices and corruption. Money lending became more and more common as productive commerce declined. Professor John Henrik Clarke, in his documentary, *A Great and Mighty Walk,* theorised that these harsh conditions helped to bring about the birth of Christianity as a reaction against harsh Roman power.

The early history of Christianity in Africa is obscure. Most of the available information comes from the Bible and thus, much of this history is controversial and contested. Outside of the Biblical information, the data is not just obscure in Africa, but is obscure everywhere else as well. One Bible story in Acts 8:26-39, however, has attracted curious attention.

> And the angel of the Lord spake unto Philip, saying, Arise, and go toward the south unto the way that goeth down from Jerusalem unto Gaza, which is desert. And he arose and went: and, behold, a man of Ethiopia, an eunuch of great authority under Candace queen of the Ethiopians, who had the charge of all her treasure, and had come to Jerusalem for to worship, Was returning, and sitting in his chariot read Esaias the prophet. Then the Spirit said unto Philip, Go near, and join thyself to this chariot. And Philip ran thither to him, and heard him read the prophet Esaias, and said, Understandest thou what thou readest? And he said, How can I, except some man should guide me? And he desired Philip that he would come up and sit with him. The place of the scripture which he read was this, He was led as a sheep to the slaughter; and like a lamb dumb

Figure 7. Map of North Africa. Numidia, Carthage and Egypt are important places in the story presented here.

> before his shearer, so opened he not his mouth: In his humiliation his judgment was taken away: and who shall declare his generation? for his life is taken from the earth. And the eunuch answered Philip, and said, I pray thee, of whom speaketh the prophet this? of himself, or of some other man? Then Philip opened his mouth, and began at the same scripture, and preached unto him Jesus. And as they went on their way, they came unto a certain water: and the eunuch said, See, here is water; what doth hinder me to be baptized? And Philip said, If thou believest with all thine heart, thou mayest. And he answered and said, I believe that Jesus Christ is the Son of God. And he commanded the chariot to stand still: and they went down both into the water, both Philip and the eunuch; and he baptized him. And when they were come up out of the water, the Spirit of the Lord caught away Philip, that the eunuch saw him no more: and he went on his way rejoicing.

The story narrates how a eunuch sent by a Queen Mother of Kush was baptised by the Apostle Philip. The name 'Candace' is really a Latinised rendering of the Kushite title 'Kentake' which means Queen or Queen Mother. Larry Williams and Charles Finch state that this individual was the first non-Jewish Christian in recorded history.

There are, however, two difficulties with this story. Firstly, we do not know which Queen or Queen Mother of Kush sent the eunuch to the Apostle Philip. It may have been Nawidemak, who ruled around 50 AD. Secondly, the archaeological evidence from Kush reveals that the mass of the population remained loyal to the traditional religion that Kush shared with Ancient Egypt, right up until the fifth century AD. It may well have been that Christianity was just a minority religion in Kush at that time.

Some say that the Apostle Thomas passed through Egypt and the Red Sea on his way to India. What do we make of this story? Professor deGraft-Johnson is of the opinion that this is doubtful. However, Professor Robert Beckford, a learned Black British theologian, believes that there is as much evidence of the Apostle Thomas evangelising in India as there is of St Peter evangelising at Rome. St Peter, by the way, is claimed to be the first Pope of Rome. If Professor Beckford is correct then the tradition of the Apostle Thomas passing through Egypt and the Red Sea (Ethiopia and Eritrea) may well be correct.

Christianity was certainly introduced into North Africa in the second century AD or before. It must still be remembered, that this region was under Roman imperial rule. Coming from Numidia (now Algeria), Namphamo is thought to be the first of the African Christian martyrs killed by the Roman establishment. Professor deGraft-Johnson quotes Professor C. P. Groves as saying: "As from this point the story of the Church in Africa unfolds before us, we find a devotion under persecution not excelled elsewhere, and a fervent fidelity to the faith expressed in Puritan ideals."

Everybody knows that the Romans killed Christians in amphitheatres. Some gruesome versions add that they fed Christians to lions. It remains a fact that many of the surviving amphitheatres of the Roman Empire are still in Africa. Moreover, lions are associated with Africa.

On 17 July 180 AD, according to Professor deGraft-Johnson, twelve African Christians were executed by the Roman controlled authorities in North Africa. Other authorities give different dates. The leader of the group was a 22 year old African woman called Perpetua. She was married and had a child. She demonstrated great courage during her execution by directing the weapon of an inexperienced gladiator against her own breast. On the ruined site of Carthage, to this day, there is a chapel dedicated to St Perpetua. Other people executed that day were Saturninus, Perpetua's brother, and a slave girl, Felicitas (also given as Felicity), who gave birth to a child just before she died.

Tertullian was another giant of the African Church. Born in Carthage around 155 AD, he studied Latin, Greek and rhetoric. Eventually, he became the head of a Church community in Carthage. However, as with many colonised peoples, he fell in love with the language of his conquerors and even became the first of the Church WRITERS to make Latin the language of Christianity. He died around the year 222 AD. At the time of his death, the African Church could boast of between 70 and 90 bishops.

During the lifetime of Tertullian, St Victor I became the first of three African Roman Popes. Professor Edward Scobie identifies St Victor I as the fourteenth Pope after St Peter. During his time in office, 189-199 AD, Victor I standardised the Celebration of Easter as the Easter Sunday. Moreover, he threatened to excommunicate the Asian Christians if they failed to fall in line. They used to hold Easter in line with the Jewish Passover. St Victor I called the First Roman Synod on record to discuss this. Finally, he was the first Pope of Rome to use Latin as the language of the MYSTERIES, replacing Greek.

Professor deGraft-Johnson narrates the story of St Cyprian. Born into a well respected family in Carthage, Cyprian experienced what he called his "heavenly birth" at the age of 46. In his younger days, he studied rhetoric. He later enjoyed a career as a professor of philosophy before he entered the church. Eventually, he rose to become the Bishop of Carthage. However, the Roman persecution of the church was gathering momentum. The crowds in the amphitheatres enjoyed seeing the Christians die. As the blood flowed, it became customary to shout: "Washed and saved!" In time, the bloodthirsty masses started calling for "The Bishop to the lions!" Cyprian went underground and escaped death for several years. He continued working as a Christian minister and wrote: "The white rose of the crown of labour might be as fair as the red rose of martyrdom." Eventually, however, things caught up with him. A death sentence was passed in 258 AD that literally called for his head. Mrs Steuart Erskine, author of *Vanished Cities of Northern Africa,* wrote: "He died magnificently, giving twenty-five pieces of gold to the executioner."

According to Professor deGraft-Johnson, Bishop Eusebius of Caesaria wrote that one of the early evangelists was an active missionary in Egypt and established churches in the Egyptian city of Alexandria. During the time of Demetrius of Alexandria 189-232 AD, there is solid evidence of a church history in that city. Demetrius appointed three bishops for the African church, Pantænus, Clement and Origen. Pantænus founded the world-famous Christian School of Alexandria, the most important centre of Christian scholarship in the world. Clement became the second head of the School and Oregon became the third head of the School. However, Professor Nnamdi Elleh, an architectural scholar, points out that the city of Alexandria, even though it was in Egypt, was built by the Greeks. He also pointed out that:

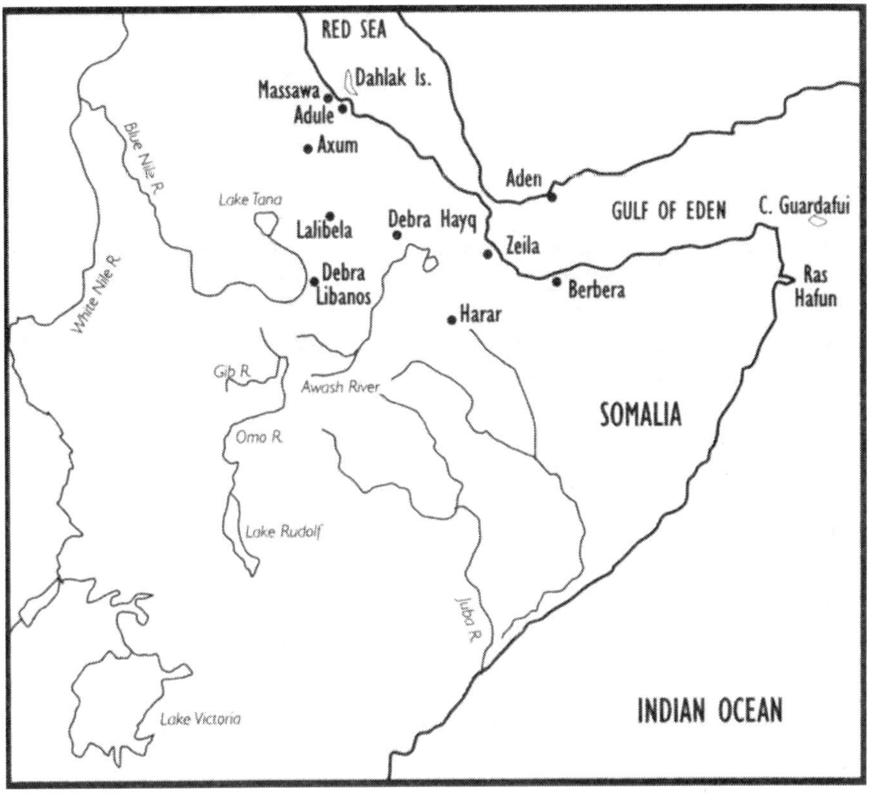

Figure 8. Map of Ethiopia and Southern Arabia. The city of Axum (also given as Aksum by some authorities) was an important centre of cultural history.

> The Ptolemaic dynasty intrinsically changed the face of Egypt from a traditional African population to its present ethnic composition. The city of Alexandria was founded on the site of an ancient Egyptian city, Raqote. Alexander the Great built his new city after his conquest … The ancient city of Alexandria is a living monument to all of humankind who were attracted to Egypt by the magnet of its wealth.

Therefore it is safe to assume that Pantænus, Clement and Origen, even though they were living in Africa, could even have been Europeans.

In Egypt of the fourth century, Professor deGraft-Johnson tells of the pioneering hermits and monks. These Desert Fathers, far to the south of Greek and Roman Alexandrian influence, were indigenous Africans. The first of the Desert Fathers was Anthony. The pioneer of the eremitic lifestyle, he sold all his earthly possessions at the age of 20 and retired to live as a hermit in the Sahara. Other people followed his example including Christians from Kush who joined his band of hermits. Anthony would become better known to history as St Anthony. Pachomius was another Egyptian Christian. He established the first Christian monastery in Upper Egypt on an island of the Nile. His followers became the first monks in history. They lived by his teachings which became known as the *Rule of Pachomius*. He would become better known to history as St Pachomius.

Ethiopia or Axum, as it was then called, was a brilliant and flourishing civilisation. Independent of Roman rule, it had a maritime trade with the Roman provinces on one hand, and China on the other. They minted gold, silver and bronze coins and boasted a literature and scripts of their own. Dr Peter Garlake, an authority on African history, wrote that "In the first half of the first millennium CE, Aksum was ranked as one of the world's greatest empires." For example, a Persian cleric of the third century identified Axum as the third most important state in the world after Persia and Rome.

Professor William Leo Hansberry, the pioneer of African studies, wrote a detailed account of how Christianity got to Ethiopia that Joseph Harris edited and published. Apparently Meropus, a Phœnician philosopher, sailed to India and was accompanied on his journey by two Syrian boys. Frumentius was the older of the two boys and Aedesius was the younger. On their return journey, their vessel, a Greco-Roman ship, was attacked as they tried to moor at an Ethiopian port. All on board were killed, except the two boys. Their age spared them. Why did this happen? Hansberry states that relations between the inhabitants of the port and the Greco-Roman sailors had recently become strained due to earlier abuses of Ethiopian hospitality. The Ethiopians sought revenge on all who could be identified as kinsfolk of the Greco-Roman merchants, hence their storming of the ship.

Eventually, the two young Syrians were taken to the Ethiopian ruler Ella Amida, Ezana's predecessor. The ruler saw potential in the boys and later installed Frumentius as his treasurer and secretary, and made Aedesius his cup-bearer. Frumentius rose to great influence within the country. When Ella Amida died, Ezana, his young son, succeeded him. The Queen-Regent invited Frumentius to assist in governing the country until the young Ezana became of age. The Syrian encouraged the spread of Christianity throughout Ethiopia, building churches and encouraging trade.

In time, Ezana assumed full control and Frumentius became Ethiopia's first bishop. The coins and inscriptions illustrate the reality of this. The

Figure 9. Coin of Emperor Ezana of Ethiopia with the Christian cross and motto: "May the country be satisfied!"

early coins of Ezana's time show the crescent-and-disk emblem of the old deity Mahrem. This was a moon deity worshipped in Ethiopia and in Yemen. The later coins issued just after 330 AD show the Christian cross with the motto: "May the country be satisfied!" These were the first coins in the world to carry this Christian design. Some writers claim that Ethiopia was the first country in the world to make Christianity the state religion. Others claim it was the second country in the world after Armenia.

Emperor Ezana commissioned the building of a very important monument in the Ethiopian capital city which was also called Axum. This building was The Cathedral of St Mary of Zion. Although this building exists today, what is standing there now is a relatively cheap rebuild. However, a Portuguese visitor to Ethiopia in around 1520 called Francisco Alvarez described the original monument in all its glory:

> In this town, we found a noble church; it is very large, and has five naves of a good width and of great length, vaulted above, and all the vaults are covered up, and the ceiling and sides are all painted; it also has a choir after our fashion. This church has a very large circuit, paved with flagstones, like gravestones, and it has also a large enclosure, and is surrounded by another large enclosure like the wall of a large town or city.

Why is this monument of such significance? Dr Georg Gerster, a Swiss art and architecture scholar, explains:

> In his history of the world, Tabari describes among other things the exile in Ethiopia of a group of Moslems. In one passage he tells of a woman who after

> her return to Mecca constantly made enthusiastic remarks about the paintings she had admired, whilst in exile, in the Cathedral of St Mary of Zion at Aksum. It hardly matters whether this is fact or fancy, a legend or the historical truth. Either way it is an indication that these Ethiopian paintings were known in early Islam and that they had a marked effect even on non-Christians. This fact is not so surprising, for modern Islamic research is more and more inclined to explain the Koran's sporadic links with Judeo-Christian tradition by pictures of the Old and New Testaments which the Prophet had seen and misinterpreted.

In other words, it was from this Cathedral in Ethiopia that the Prophet Muhammad, the founder of Islam, learned stories from the Judaeo-Christian tradition that appear in the Koran. As we shall see in the later part of this book, Ethiopia, or Axum, as it was then called, was important to the history of Islam for additional reasons.

After years of persecuting the Christians, a Roman ruler converted to Christianity in AD 312. Emperor Constantine I became the first Christian Roman Emperor. What is less known, however, is that the Pope of Rome during the Emperor's conversion was the second of the three African Popes. St Miltiades was in office between 311 and 314 AD. Professor Scobie identifies him as the thirty-second Pope after St Peter. St Augustine said of him: "an excellent pontiff, a true son of peace and father of Christians."

Emperor Constantine I aimed to make Christianity the state religion of the Roman Empire. However, there was a major dispute between two African church dignitaries in the city of Alexandria, Egypt. The dignitaries were Arius and Athanasius. Although they are described as Africans, being from the city of Alexandria, we cannot be sure of their real ethnicity. In any case, Constantine called the Nicene Conference of the Bishops in 325 AD to solve the dispute (and to create Roman Catholicism). Arius taught that Jesus had one nature only and that was divine--this was called Monophysitism. This doctrine spread even into Central Europe. The followers of Arius were called Arians. However, Athanasius taught that Jesus was fully man and fully God--a doctrine that was eventually accepted and became part of the Nicene Creed. The African followers of Athanasius were called Melkites.

The Nicene Conference ended in 332 AD. The outcomes were controversial and the scholars do not agree on what these outcomes were. My research suggests that the Bible was canonised. This meant that the bishops agreed on which scrolls were going in and which ones were coming out. The result of this was the creation of the *Helios Biblios* or Holy Bible that we have today. *Helios Biblios,* of course, means Sun Books. A

Figure 10. Etching of the Cathedral of St Mary of Zion in Axum.

manuscript was produced that dates back to that time which became the prototype Bible (the *Codex Vaticanus*). The New Testament books that did not make it into the Holy Bible were put aside into another collection of manuscripts that became known as the New Testament Apocrypha. The chief outcome of this conference was that Roman Catholicism was born. However, the Orthodox Churches were the first to disregard Roman Catholic influence and produce their own theology. It was only within the last 500 years that the Protestant Churches came into existence following the teachings of Martin Luther. They also disregarded Roman Catholic influence.

Professor deGraft-Johnson wrote a very upbeat account of the last of the great African Christians, St Augustine. Described as the greatest of the post Nicene Fathers, Augustine was born in Tagaste in the province of Numidia 15 November 354 AD. One scholar described him as the greatest figure in the last days of Roman rule in North Africa. Professor Charles Finch described him as the greatest Christian theologian after St Paul. His autobiography, the *Confessions,* is considered amongst the greatest autobiographies ever written, up there with Samuel Pepys and Jean-Jacques Rousseau. Professor deGraft-Johnson quotes a passage from an English historian Jane Soames, where she says: "St Augustine is far more comprehensible to a European audience today than our contemporary North African authors--a fact which is in striking disproof of modern racial theories." This is an important point. At the time that she wrote this, racist theories and extreme right wing politics were spreading across Europe. Soames is reminding us that a modern European will be able to relate a lot more to St Augustine's writings, even though he was an African, than they will be able to relate to North African writers of today, even though the North Africans today are largely Caucasoids.

What do we know about St Augustine? Augustine's mother was St Monica, a pious Christian, with aristocratic prejudices. However, his father, Patricius, was a pagan. There is some speculation amongst Catholic sources that Augustine's father could have been a Roman. I do not know if this is true. Whichever be the case, his father sent him to school in the city of Madauros, Numidia, where he studied Latin writers and came to consider Latin as his second language. He also studied Greek but found it difficult. At school, the young Augustine prayed to be saved from the whippings, but those prayers went unanswered. After leaving school, he completed his studies in Carthage, a city he describes as a sink of iniquity. However Augustine makes it clear that he was part of that iniquity. In Carthage, he gambled and frequented the amphitheatre.

At the age of 28, he left for Italy. In the city of Milan, he converted to Christianity, perhaps influenced by St Ambrose. He later taught rhetoric in Milan and also in Rome. However, following the death of his mother, he returned to Africa with the ambition of setting up a monastery and shutting himself off from the cares and temptations of the world. Instead, he was appointed bishop of Hippo where he went on to write *City of God* and *Confessions.*

City of God was written to contextualise Christianity against the charge that it was responsible for the decline of Roman power. In the book, St Augustine makes the following claims. Man is a citizen of two cities, the city of his birth and the city of God. On the one side stands the earthly city --appetitive and possessing impulses of the lower human nature. It is the Kingdom of Satan represented by the pagan empires of Assyria and Rome.

This civilisation is temporary as all earthly kingdoms are temporary. On the other side stands the Kingdom of Christ, founded on heavenly peace and spiritual salvation. This is represented by the Hebrew nation and ultimately the Church. This civilisation is permanent.

The *Confessions* contains his autobiographical information. The spiritual message of the book can be summed up in one sentence: "Oh Lord, give me chastity but not yet!"

St Augustine also wrote a very interesting passage that has attracted the interest of J. A. Rogers and the erudite African-American historian Professor John G. Jackson. St Augustine wrote: "That which is known as the Christian religion existed among the ancients, and never did not exist; from the beginning of the human race until the time when Christ came in the flesh, at which time the true religion, which already existed began to be called Christianity." What does this strange passage mean? We will attempt to answer this in the next chapter.

Following the death of St Augustine, the African Church faced grave challenges. The most devastating challenge came from the Vandal invasion of North Africa in the fifth century AD. The Vandals were one of a number of Germanic speaking peoples who exploded onto the world scene in the fifth century, destroying the Roman Empire. Some of these Germanic speakers, the Angles, Saxons and Jutes, conquered their way into Britain and became the English of today. Another group, the Franks, conquered their way into France and became the French of today. Another group, the Visigoths conquered their way into Spain and became the Spanish of today. The Vandals that conquered North Africa destroyed a lot of North African people and Christian heritage and became a segment of the Berbers of today.

The Byzantine Empire reconquered North Africa from the Vandals, and, according to the sources, killed millions in the process. The Byzantines also spread Christianity to early Mediaeval Nubia for political reasons. I describe this Nubian church history in my book *When We Ruled,* Chapter 16. This was followed by the Arabian Invasion of North Africa (639-708 AD) which brought Islam into Africa and mostly buried the early Christian heritage. The Arabs also fully displaced the indigenous Black people of North Africa. Only in Ethiopia did the early Church thrive in anything approaching an African image.

What did the Ethiopians believe? Sir E. A. Wallis Budge wrote a useful two-volume text called *A History of Ethiopia, Nubia & Abyssinia.* The book is far from perfect, and contains a marked anti-Negro tone

Figure 11. 1520 AD Manuscript of the Bible. Written in Ethiopic, it is known as the *Gunda Gunde Gospels.*

throughout. However it does contain useful information that can be extracted especially pages 156 to 159.

Ethiopian Bibles contain Old Testament books that Catholics may recognise but Protestants do not use. These include: The Books of Maccabees, The Shepherd of Hermas, The Ascension of Isaiah, The Book of Baruch, Tobit, Judith, Ecclesiasticus, The Book of Wisdom, The Epistle of Jeremiah, The Book of Adam and Eve, The Book of Enoch, Kufale, Reliqua Verborum Baruchi, The Prophecy of Jeremiah to Pashur, Susanna, Song of the Three Holy Children, and Bel and the Dragon. The Ethiopian Bible is the only one today that has a complete version of The Book of Enoch.

The Ethiopians traditionally believed that God is one and triune. They teach that Jesus was Divine and his human nature was absorbed into the Divine nature reflecting the belief of the Arians described in the last chapter. They also teach that the Virgin Mary is the "Mother of God." This elevated status for the Virgin Mary, is higher than the status given to the Virgin by Catholics and much higher than the status given by the Protestants. Moreover, it is because of this Ethiopian belief that the Koran (Sura 5:116) incorrectly teaches that Christianity as a whole believe in a

Trinity composed of God the Father, Mary and Jesus. Finally, the Ethiopians believe and accept the idea of Angels, Archangels, and Guardian Angels. This may reflect ancient Nile Valley influence.

What happens to the soul after death? Ethiopians traditionally believe that the souls of the blessed do not go immediately to Paradise. They abide in a place of peace and rest awaiting the Last Judgement. However, the souls of the wicked have no abiding place but wander distractedly. It is the Last Judgement that decides who goes to Heaven or Hell.

Fasting is an important part of the Ethiopian calendar. It was customary to have fasts every Wednesday and Friday before noon. Other fasts were for Lent, The Ninevah Fast (3 days in February), The Advent Fast (40 days), The Fast of the Apostles (15 days), The Fast of the Assumption (15 days in August), The Fast of Kueskuam (40 days in October and November), the Vigil at Christmas and the Vigil at Epiphany. It is important to note that not all fasts were for the whole day!

The Ethiopians celebrated various festivals throughout the year celebrating the birth of Jesus, His incarnation, His baptism, His passion, His transfiguration, His Ascension, et cetera. They also celebrated various festivals celebrating the conception of Mary, Her Nativity, the entry into the temple, the building of Her church, the consecration of Her church, Her appearance in Egypt, Her death, and Her Assumption, et cetera.

Many Ethiopian religious practices come from Judaism. The dietary laws associated with kosher are practised by Ethiopians. The practice of circumcision (and female circumcision) is also practised. The separation of men and women in the church replicates the separation of men and women in the synagogue. The Ethiopians revere the Sabbath, unlike most Christians. Finally Ethiopian churches have The Tabot, which are replicas of the Ark of the Covenant.

CHAPTER TWO: THE BIBLICAL JESUS/CHRIST

St Augustine's suggestion that Christianity always existed and never did not exist may have a very specific meaning, missed by most Christians. The great African Father may have been referring to similarities in ideas and doctrines between Christianity and much older religions. The Reverend Dr Martin Luther King, easily the greatest Christian theologian of the twentieth century, recognised the same thing in his student days. In 1949 he wrote an essay called *A Study of Mithraism,* where he said:

> The Greco-Roman world in which the early church developed was one of diverse religions ... The people of that age were eager and zealous in their search for religious experience. The existence of this atmosphere was vitally important in the development and eventual triumph of Christianity. These many religions were not alike in every respect; to draw this conclusion would lead to a gratuitous and erroneous supposition. But it is to be noticed that they possessed many fundamental likenesses; (1) All held that the initiate shared in symbolic (sacramental) fashion the experiences of the god. (2) All had secret rites for the initiated. (3) All offered mystical cleansing from sin. (4) All promised a happy future life for the faithful. It is not at all surprising in view of the wide and growing influence of these religions that when the disciples in Antioch and elsewhere preached a crucified and risen Jesus they should be regarded as the heralds of another mystery religion ... It is at this point that we are able to see why knowledge of these cults is important for any serious New Testament study. It is well-nigh impossible to grasp Christianity through and through without knowledge of these cults. That there were striking similarities between the developing church and these religions cannot be denied. Even Christian apologist[s] had to admit that fact ... This is not to say that a Saint Paul or a Saint John sat down and copied these views verbatim. But after being in contact with these surrounding religions and hearing certain doctrines expressed, it was only natural for some of these views to become a part of their subconscious minds. When they sat down to write they were expressing consciously that which had dwelled in their subconscious minds. It is also significant to know that Roman tolerance had favoured this great syncretism of religious ideas. Borrowing was not only natural but inevitable. One of the most interesting of these ancient cults was Mithraism, which bore so many points of resemblance to Christianity that it is a challenge to the modern student to investigate these likenesses and learn more about them.

Dr Robert Beckford, a learned Black British professor of Theology, made a radical documentary called *The Hidden Story of Jesus*. One of the academics Professor Beckford interviewed was Egyptologist Dr Bojana Mojsov. She contributed the following information:

> Well, once a year there was a Festival of Osiris. And the myth of Osiris is the most ancient myth of Egypt. The Festival lasted for about a week and reached its culmination on the last three days. And on the first of those three days, the earth body of Osiris would be buried. During the second day, vigils in the temple were said for the god's resurrection. And then on the morning of the third day, the statue was brought out into the court ... and all the pilgrims who will have gathered from all over Egypt celebrated the resurrection of Osiris.

A number of scholars have explored similar ideas in their respective books since the eighteenth century. The French Enlightenment scholar, Charles Dupuis, wrote *On the Origin of All Religious Worship*. Originally written in the late eighteenth century, an abridged version of it appeared in New Orleans in 1872. His disciple, Count de Volney, wrote *The Ruins of Empires* also at the end of the eighteenth century. De Volney learned English and translated the book himself from the original French in 1802. This book is one of the glories of Enlightenment literature. The two French pioneers influenced the English magistrate Godfrey Higgins Esq, who wrote the exceptionally erudite two volume text *Anacalypsis* in 1836. This book would influence Major-General J. G. R. Forlong to write the two volume *Rivers of Life* in 1883 (published in London by Bernard Quaritch), quite possibly the most erudite and difficult book this present author has ever seen. The Reverend Charles H. Vail, an American churchman, wrote *The World's Saviours* in 1913 (published in London by Fowler). Finally, Dr Albert Churchward wrote *The Origin and Evolution of Religion* in 1924 (published in London by George Allen & Unwin Ltd.). This book represents a summary of the findings of the previous writers.

Most of Albert Churchward's research on the origins of Christianity is derived from the research of his mentor Gerald Massey. Gerald Massey is little known today but his reputation has been kept alive, strangely enough, in the Black community, having been cited by Mr J. A. Rogers, Professor Yosef ben-Jochannan and Professor John G. Jackson. Professor Charles Finch has also drawn heavily on Massey's research. Massey's most famous work today is the two volume text, *Ancient Egypt: The Light of the World*. Massey claims that a comparison between the Ancient Egyptian belief system and later religions shows fruitful comparisons since the later religions have borrowed from the earlier ones. With respect to Christianity, he demonstrates this on pages 690 to 905 of Volume 2.

Establishment 'scholars' have been unable to contain their anger at Massey. Wikipedia at the time of writing dismisses his work as pseudohistory. However, the best they have ever been able to do, is to simply lie about Massey's findings and refute the strawman arguments that they themselves have constructed. Another strategy is to find establishment scholars of doubtful academic integrity who are prepared to make mendacious claims. They have not been able to refute Massey's actual work.

I will present Massey's own summary of his work taken from the Appendix of Volume 2, i.e. pages 907 to 914.

EGYPTIAN = CHRISTIAN

The Mysteries =The miracles.

The Sem, or mythical representations = The parables.

The Ritual [i.e. Book of the Dead] as the book of resurrection = The Book of Revelation.

The sayings of Iu or Iu-em-hetep = The Sayings of Jesus.

Huhi the father in heaven as the eternal, a title of Atum-Ra = Ihuh, the father in heaven as the eternal.

Ra, the holy spirit = God the Holy Ghost.

Ra the father of Iu the Su, or son of God, with the hawk or dove as the bird of the holy spirit = God, the Father of Jesus, with the dove as the bird of the Holy Spirit.

Iu or Horus, the manifesting son of God = Jesus the manifesting Son of God.

The trinity of Atum (or Osiris) the father, Horus (or Iu) the son, and Ra the holy spirit = The Trinity of the Father, Son and Holy Spirit.

Iu-Su or Iusa, the coming son of Iusaas, who was great with Iusa or Iusu = Jesus.

The ever-coming Messu or Child as Egyptian = The Hebrew Messianic Child.

Horus (or Heru), the Lord by name, as a child = Child-Jesus as the Lord by name (Gospels of the Infancy).

Isis, the virgin mother of Iu, her Su or son = Mary the virgin mother of Jesus.

The first Horus as Child of the Virgin, the second as son of Ra, the father = Jesus the Virgin's child, the Christ as son of the father

The first Horus as the founder, the second as fulfiller for the father = Jesus as the founder, and the Christ as fulfiller for the father.

The two mothers of Child-Horus, Isis and Nephthys, who were two sisters = The two mothers of Child-Jesus, who were sisters.

Meri or Nut, the mother-heaven = Mary as Regina Cœli.

The outcast great mother with her seven sons = Mary Magdalene, with her seven devils.

Isis taken by Horus in adultery with Sut = The woman taken in adultery.

Apt, the crib or manger, by name as the birthplace and mother in one = The manger as cradle of the Child-Christ.

Seb, the earth-father, as consort to the virgin Isis = Joseph, the father on earth, as putative husband to the Virgin Mary.

Seb, the foster-father to Child-Horus = Joseph, as foster-father to the Child-Jesus.

Seb, Isis and Horus, the Kamite holy trinity = Joseph, Mary and Jesus, a Christian holy trinity.

Seb, the builder of the house, the carpenter = Joseph, the carpenter.

Seb, the custodian of the mummied dead = Joseph of Arimathea, the keeper of the Corpus Christi.

Sut and Horus, the twin opponents = Satan and Jesus, the twin opponents.

Horus, the sower, and Sut, the destroyer, in the harvest-field = Jesus, the sower of the good seed, and Satan, the sower of tares.

Sut and Horus contending in the desert = Satan and Jesus contending in the wilderness.

Sut and Horus contending on the Ben-Ben or Pyramidion = Satan and Jesus contending on the pinnacle.

Horus carried off by Sut to the summit of Mount Hetep = Jesus spirited away by Satan into an exceeding high mountain.

Sut and Horus contending on the mount = Satan and Jesus contending on the mount.

Sut undoing the good that Horus does = Satan sowing tares by night.

S'men, for Khemen, a title of Taht = Simeon.

S'men, who held Child-Horus in his arms as the young solar god = Simeon, who took the Child-Jesus in his arms.

Anna or Annit (a title of Hathor), with Taht-S'men = Anna, the prophetess, with Simeon.

The Petar or Petra by name in Egyptian as Revealer to Horus = Peter, the revealer to the Christ.

The house of Annu = Bethany.

The group in the house at Annu = The group in the house at Bethany.

Horus in Annu = Jesus in Bethany.

Asar or Osiris = Lazarus.

The two sisters Mertae = The two sisters Mary and Martha.

Osiris, whom Horus loved = Lazarus, whom Jesus loved.

Osiris perfumed for his burial = Jesus anointed, when the odour fills the house.

Osiris prays that he may be buried speedily = Jesus begs that his death may be effected quickly.

Osiris prepared for burial under the hair of Hathor-Meri = Jesus prepared for his burial beneath the hair of Mary

Osiris, who slept in the tomb at Annu = Lazarus, who slept in the tomb at Bethany.

Osiris raised from the tomb by Horus in Annu = Lazarus raised from the tomb at Bethany.

The mummy Osiris bidden to come forth by Horus = The mummy Lazarus bidden to come forth by Jesus

The Great One who does the work of washing = Jesus washing the feet of his disciples.

The star, as announcer for the Child-Horus = The Star in the East that indicated the birthplace of Jesus.

The seven Hathors (or cows) who minister to Horus = The seven women who minister to Jesus.

Anup, the Precursor of Horus = John, the forerunner of Jesus the Christ.

Anup, the Baptizer = John the Baptist.

Aan, the saluter of Horus = John, the saluter of the Christ.

Aan, a name of the divine scribe = John, the divine scribe.

Hermes, the scribe = Hermas, the scribe.

Mati, the registrar = Matthew, the clerk.

Taht, Shu, and black Sut = The three kings, or Magi.

Nut at the pool of the Persea, or sycamore-tree, as giver of divine drink = The woman at the well as giver of the water.

Horus born in Annu, the place of bread = Jesus born in Bethlehem, the house of bread.

The vesture put on Horus by the Goddess Tait = The swaddling clothes put on the infant Jesus.

Offerings made to the child by the worshippers in Annu = Offerings and worship of the Magi.

Child-Horus with the head of Ra = Child-Jesus with the solar glory round his head.

The Bull of Amenta in the place of birth = The ox in the birthplace of the Child.

The ass, Iu, in the birthplace = The ass in the birthplace (catacombs).

The lions of the horizon attending upon Horus = The lions attending the Child-Christ (pseudo-Matthew).

Child-Horus emerging from the Papyrus-reed = The Child-Jesus in the catacombs issuing from the Papyrus.

Horus, the ancient child = The little old Jesus in the catacombs.

Horus, the gracious child = Jesus, the child full of grace.

Horus, one of five brethren = Jesus, one of five brothers.

Horus, the brother of Sut the betrayer = Jesus, the brother of Judas the betrayer.

Amsta, the one brother of Horus in the human form = James, the human brother of Jesus.

The two sisters of Horus = The sisters of Jesus.

Horus the lad in the country and youth in town = Jesus as the child in the country and youth in town.

Horus baptized with water by Anup = Jesus baptized with water by John.

Horus in the tank of flame = Jesus the baptizer with fire.

Horus in his baptism becoming the beloved Son of God the Father = Jesus becoming the Son of God the Father in his baptism.

Horus the husbandman with the fan in his hand = Christ coming with the fan in his hand.

Horus the Good Shepherd, with the crook upon his shoulder = Jesus the Good Shepherd, with the lamb or kid upon his shoulder.

Horus with the four followers in the Mount = Jesus with the four disciples in the Mount.

Horus with the seven great spirits in the Mount = Jesus with the seven spirits in the Mount (Rev.).

Herrut the Apap-reptile, slayer of the younglings in the egg = Herod, the murderer of the innocents.

Isis commanded to take her child down into Egypt for safety = Mary warned to take her Child down into Egypt for safety.

Horus as the typical fish = Jesus as Ichthus the fish.

Horus as the fisher = Jesus as the fisher.

The four fishers with Horus as founders of the kingdom = The four fishers with Jesus as founders of the kingdom.

Sebek, the father of the fishers = Zebedee, the father of the fishers.

Two fisher-brethren, Kabhsenuf and Hapi = Two fisher-brethren, Simon and Andrew.

Two other fisher-brethren, Amsta and Tuamutef = Two other fisher-brethren, James and John.

The seven on board the bark with Horus = The seven fishers on board the bark with Jesus.

The wonderful net of the fishers = The miraculous draught of fishes in the net.

Horus as the lamb = Jesus as the lamb.

Horus as the lion = Jesus as a lion.

Horus (Iu) as the black child = Jesus as the little black bambino.

Horus as Ahi, the striker with the flabellum = Jesus wielding the scourge of cords as the striker.

Horus identified with the Tat or Cross = Jesus identified with the Cross.

The blind Horus, in two characters, as the God and Manes = The two blind men of the Gospels.

Horus of twelve years = Jesus of twelve years.

Horus made a man of thirty years in his baptism = Jesus, the man of thirty years in his baptism

Horus (Iu), the son of a beetle = Jesus, the good Scarabaeus.

Horus (or Ra) as the great cat = Jesus as the cat.

Horus as the shrewmouse = The mouse of Jesus dedicated to "Our Lady."

Horus, the healer in the mountain = Jesus, the healer in the mountain.

Horus as Iusa, the exorcizer of evil spirits as the Word = Jesus, the caster out of demons with a word.

Horus, born as the shoot, branch, or plant from the Nun = Jesus born as the Natzer of Nazareth, so rendered in the course of localizing the legend.

Osiris as the vine-plant, Aarru = Jesus as the vine.

Horus, the bringer of the fish and the grapes in Egypt = Jesus as bringer of the fish and the grapes (catacombs).

Horus, the child standing on two crocodiles which adore him = The Christ-Child adored by dragons=crocodiles.

Horus, the child of a widow = The Child-Christ who lodges with a widow in Egypt.

Horus, the child of the widow in Sutenkhen = The Child-Christ with the widow in Sotenin (pseudo-Matthew).

The golden Horus = The corn-complexioned Jesus.

Horus full of wine = Jesus the wine-bibber.

Horus, who gives the water of life = Jesus as giver of the water of life.

Horus in the lentils and the grain = Jesus the bread of life.

Horus as Unbu in the bush of thorn = Jesus in the crown of thorn.

Horus the just and true = Jesus the faithful and true.

Horus-Mat-Kheru, the Word made truth at the second coming = Jesus the spirit of truth at the Second Advent.

The human Horus glorified in becoming a (Khu) spirit = The spirit not given until Jesus is glorified.

The world made through Horus = The world made through Jesus.

Horus the bridegroom with the bride in Sothis = Jesus the bridegroom with the bride.

Horus of both sexes = Jesus as the bearded Sophia; Charis, the female Christ.

Horus who exalteth his father in every sacred place = Jesus who exalteth his father in every place.

Horus as Remi the weeper = Jesus as the weeper.

Dumb Horus, or the silent Sekari = Jesus silent before his accusers.

Horus behaving badly to Isis = Jesus speaking brutally to his mother.

Horus the gladsome = Jesus the jocund.

Horus as prince of the divine powers = Jesus the prince.

Horus the uplifted serpent = Jesus uplifted as the serpent.

Horus as the Bennu = Jesus as the phoenix.

Horus who giveth light by means of his own body = Jesus the light of the world.

Horus the hider of himself as Har-Sheta = Jesus the concealer of himself.
Horus the word-made-flesh = Jesus the word-made-flesh.
Horus the word-made-truth = Jesus the doer of the word.
Horus in the bosom of Ra = Jesus in the bosom of the Father.
Horus the Krst = Jesus the Christ.
Horus the avenger = Jesus who brings the sword.
Iu-em-hetep who comes with peace = Jesus the bringer of peace.
Horus called the illegitimate child = Jesus called the Mamzer.
Horus the afflicted one = Jesus the afflicted one.
Horus the unique one = Jesus the unique one.
Horus the lord of resurrections from the house of death = Jesus the resurrection and the life.
Horus as the type of life eternal = Jesus the type of eternal life.
Iu (em-hetep) the child-teacher in the temple = The Child-Jesus as teacher in the Temple.
Child-Horus as sower of the seed = Child-Jesus as sower of the seed.
Har-Khuti, lord of the harvest = Jesus, lord of the harvest.
Horus the founder = Jesus the founder.
Horus the fulfiller = Jesus the fulfiller.
Horus as master of the words of power = Jesus whose word was with power.
Horus Ma-kheru = Jesus, "the witness unto the truth."
Horus as the lily = Jesus typified by the lily.
Horus the link = Jesus the bond of union.
Horus who came to fulfil the law = Jesus who comes to fulfil the law.
Horus as bearer of the Ankh-symbol of life and the Un-sceptre of resurrection = Jesus as the resurrection and the life personified.
Horus (or Khunsu) the chaser of boastfulness = Jesus the humbler of the proud.
Horus of the Second Advent = The coming Christ.
Horus the hidden force = Jesus the concealed.
Horus as Kam-Ura, the overflower, and extender of the water illimitably = Jesus, giver of the water of life without limit.
Horus, who came by the water, the blood and the spirit = Jesus, who came by the water, the blood and the spirit.
Horus the opener as Unen = Jesus the opener with the keys.
Horus of the two horizons = Jesus of the two lands.
Horus as teacher of the living generation = Jesus as teacher on the earth.
Horus as teacher of the spirits in Amenta = Jesus as preacher to the spirits in prison.
Horus as teacher on the Atit-bark, with the seven glorious ones on board = Jesus the teacher on the boat, also with the seven fishers on board.
Horus uttering the words of Ra in the solar bark = Jesus uttering the parables on board the boat.
Horus walking the water = Jesus walking the water.
The blind mummy made to see by Horus = The blind man given sight by Jesus.
Horus and the Hamemmet or younglings of Shu = Jesus and the little ones.
The children of Horus = The children of Jesus.
Horus the raiser of the dead = Jesus the raiser of the dead.
Horus the raiser up of Asar = Jesus the raiser up of Lazarus.
Horus, who imparts the power of the resurrection to his children = Jesus who confers the same power on his followers.

Horus entering the mount at sunset to hold converse with his father = Jesus entering the mount at sunset to hold converse with his father.

Horus one with the father = Jesus one with his father.

Horus transfigured on the mount = Jesus transfigured on the mount.

Amsu-Horus in his resurrection as a Sahu-mummy = Jesus rising again corporeally or incorporated.

The blood of Isis = The issue of blood suffered by the woman.

The field manured with blood in Tattu = Aceldama.

The mummy-bandage that was woven without seam = The vesture of the Christ without a seam.

Seven souls of Ra the Holy Spirit = Seven gifts of the Holy Spirit.

Seven hawks of Ra the Holy Spirit = Seven doves of the Holy Spirit.

Seven loaves of Horus for feeding the multitude reposing in the green fields of Annu = Seven loaves of Jesus for feeding the multitude reclining on the grass.

Twelve followers of Har-Khuti = Twelve followers of Jesus, as the twelve disciples.

Horus with the twelve in the field of divine harvest = Jesus with the twelve in the harvest-field.

The twelve who reap for Horus = The twelve who reap for Jesus.

Horus as the intercessor = Jesus as the paraclete.

Horus as the great judge = Jesus as the great judge.

The judgment of the righteous, who are the sheep of Horus, the good shepherd = Judgment of the righteous, who are the sheep of Jesus the Good Shepherd.

The judgment of the guilty, who are the goats of Sut = Judgment of the wicked, who are the goats of Satan.

Horus parting off the evil dead = Jesus parting off the accursed.

The condemned spirits entering the swine = The evil spirits entering the swine.

The glorious ones that wait on Horus = The angels that minister unto Jesus.

Horus ascending to heaven from Bakhu, the Mount of the olive tree = Jesus ascending to heaven from Mount Olivet.

The revelation of Horus, given by Ra, his father, to make known the mysteries of divine things to his followers = The revelation of Jesus Christ which God gave him to show unto his servants.

The revelation written down by Aan (Tehuti), the scribe of divine words = The Revelation written by John the divine.

The saluter Aani, who bears witness to the word of Ra and to the testimony of Horus = John, who bears witness to the Word of God and the testimony of Jesus Christ.

The secret of the Mysteries revealed by Taht-Aan = The secret of the Mysteries made known by John.

The books in Annu = The book of doom and the book of life in Patmos.

The books and their bringer = The book and its opener.

Seven dungeon-seals = The book with seven seals.

The great mother Apt, the pregnant water-cow = The woman sitting on the waters.

The crocodile as great mother = The dragon as great mother.

The great mother as Hathor, the abode = The woman that was the great city personalized.

The great or enceinte mother in her lunar character = The woman arrayed with the sun about to bring forth the child

Isis, who brought forth Horus in the marshes = The woman who brought forth in the wilderness.

Isis pursued by the great crocodile = The woman persecuted by the dragon.

Isis, hawk-winged = The woman with eagle's wings.

The bride as Hathor-Isis, with the calf or lamb upon the mount of glory = The bride as the lamb's wife upon the mount.

Atum-Huhi, the closer and the opener of Amenta = Ihuh, who carries the keys of death and Hades as closer and opener.

Atum-Ra, the holy spirit = The spirit.

Hathor-Iusaas the bride, with Horus the lamb (or earlier calf) upon the mount = The bride with the lamb upon the mount.

Anup and Aan, the two witnesses for Horus = The two Johns as witnesses for Jesus.

The seven Khuti or glorious ones = The seven spirits of God.

Horus, with the seven Khabsu stars, or gods of the lamp = Jesus in the midst of the seven golden lamp-stands.

Sebek-Horus the lamb on the mount = Jesus the lamb on the mount.

Horus the morning star = Jesus the morning star.

Horus, who gives the morning star to his followers = Jesus, who gives the morning star to his followers.

The Har-Seshu, or servants of Horus = The servants of Jesus Christ.

The seven spirits of fire around the throne of Ra = The seven spirits of fire before the throne.

The fathers, or the ancient ones = The four-and-twenty elders.

The four corner-keepers = The four living creatures at the four corners.

The solar god of golden form = The form with feet like unto burnished brass, and countenance as of the sun.

Iu the son of man (or Atum) = Jesus the son of man.

Horus as the first-born from the dead = Jesus the Christ as first-born of those that slept.

Horus in the house of a thousand years = The Millennial reign of Jesus.

Sebek the solar dragon = The scarlet-coloured beast with seven heads.

Seven souls or powers of Ra = Seven heads of the solar dragon.

The eighth to the seven = The eighth to the seven.

Ten Tata-gods or powers = The ten horns or kings.

The war in heaven = The war in heaven.

Har-Tema as the avenger, the red god who orders the block of execution = The word of God, faithful and true, with raiment dipped in blood.

Har-Makhu = Michael the Archangel.

Sut the accuser = Satan the accuser.

Sut and Horus = Christ and the Anti-Christ.

The celestial Heptanomis = The seven mountains of earth or islands in the sea.

The seven children of the old earth-mother = The seven kings of the earth.

Horus at the head of the seven = Jesus at the head of the seven.

The last judgment = The last judgment.

The mount of glory = The throne set in heaven on the mount.

The mount as judgment-seat = The mount as throne of the Great Judge.

The lion-faced throne of steel = The great white throne.

The great judge seated on his throne = The Great Judge on the judgment-seat.

The god in lion form = The god who is the lion of the Tribe of Judah.

The god in the solar disc = The god with the sun-like countenance.

The god whose dazzling mouth sends forth breezes of flame = The god from whose mouth proceeded the two-edged sword.

Osiris-Tat, the sufferer in the Lower Egypt of Amenta = The Lord who was crucified in Egypt.

The Apap-reptile, the serpent of evil = Abaddon, Apollyon, or Satan, that old serpent.

Apap, the power of evil in the Abyss = Abaddon or Apollyon, the angel of the Abyss.

The binding of Apap in chains and casting the beast into the Abyss = The binding of the dragon, that old serpent, and casting him into the Pit.

Apap and Sut bound in chains and cast into the Abyss = The Devil and Satan bound in a great chain and cast into the Pit.

The Ankh-key of life and the Un-symbol of the resurrection = The keys of death and Hades in the hands of the opener.

The first resurrection and the second death in Amenta = The first resurrection and the second death.

The Lake of Putrata where the lost souls fall headlong into everlasting night = The lake of the second death.

The beatified in their white garments of glory = The beatified spirits arrayed in white.

The name of Ra on the head of the deceased = The name of the Father written on the forehead.

The little column of white stone given as a talisman to the initiates = The white stone given to the initiated.

The mount of the double earth in Hetep = The mountain great and high.

The eternal city at the summit = The Holy City.

The water of life as lake or river = The river of the water of life.

The two divine sycamores over the water of life = The tree of life on either side of the water of life.

The water of life proceeding from the throne of Osiris = The water of life proceeding from the throne of God.

The great lake in Hetep upon which the gods and glorified alight = The glassy sea on which the victors stand triumphant.

The great white lake of Sa = The sea of crystal.

The calf (later lamb) of Horus standing on the mount with Hathor bearing the bride = The lamb standing on Mount Zion with the bride.

The lunar goddess Hathor bearing the solar orb = The woman arrayed with the sun, and the moon at her feet.

The glorified in Hetep stoled and girdled and crowned = The angels girt about the breasts with golden girdles.

The emerald dawn around the mount or throne of Ra = The rainbow like an emerald round the throne.

The Ba enclosure of Aarru, in twelve measures = The walled enclosure of the New Jerusalem, in twelve measures.

Heaven according to the measure of a man = Heaven according to the measure of a man.

The paradise of the pole-star = The Holy City lighted by one luminary that is neither the sun nor the moon=the pole-star.

The ark of Osiris-Ra = The Ark of the New Covenant in heaven

What should we make of the similarities? In my judgement, there are clearly errors in this analysis but this is NOT the same as saying that it is ALL in error. Professor Charles Finch in *Echoes of the Old Darkland,* pages 179 to 216, corrects and improves on portions of this. There are also many examples where Massey uses old forms of the Ancient Egyptian names that scholars now spell very differently. Moreover, Massey has stressed the similarities between the Egyptian and Christian examples. He has not stressed the differences enough. To illustrate the point, suppose there are 500 key points in the Christ story and 500 key points in the Horus story. Massey has presented 200 similarities. This still means that there are 300 differences. Secondly, I believe that many of his similarities can be condensed into, for the sake of argument, 100 similarities. This may mean that there are 100 similarities and 400 differences.

How do we interpret this? I believe that to over stress the similarities can easily cloud one's understanding of Christianity. It also clouds one's understanding of the Ancient Egyptian belief system. However, to ignore the similarities altogether, as some scholars are more comfortable doing, is simply not a scholarly approach, even if the differences outweigh the similarities. Nor is it scholarly to pretend that Massey's work is lacking in the necessary scholarly rigour when it CLEARLY IS a work of rigorous scholarship.

My own position is in line with St Augustine and the Reverend Dr Martin Luther King. We must accept that the similarities between Christianity and older religious ideas, such as the religion of the Ancient Egyptians do exist and are real. We also have to accept that newer religions borrow from earlier religions as a standard practice even if the later religions have new and different theological aims.

CHAPTER THREE: THE HISTORICAL JESUS (JOSHUA)

Many scholars, in the light of the Massey evidence, have posed a very challenging question: Did Jesus of Nazareth actually exist as a flesh-and-blood historical personage?

The Roman Jewish historian, Josephus, wrote the *Antiquities of the Jews,* quoted on page 215 of Charles Finch's, *Echoes of the Old Darkland.* There is a passage in that text that many scholars believe is questionable indeed that read as follows:

> Now, there was about this time, Jesus, a wise man, if it be lawful to call him a man, for he was a doer of wonderful works,--a teacher of such men as receive the truth with pleasure. He drew over to him both many of the Jews, and many of the Gentiles. He was (the) Christ; and when Pilate ... had condemned him to the cross, those that loved him at the first did not forsake him for he appeared to them alive again the third day, as the divine prophets had foretold.

This passage, if authentic, would have greatly supported the historicity of Jesus. However, Professor John G. Jackson in *Pagan Origins of the Christ Myth,* says: "it is generally regarded as a forgery, even by Christian scholars."

Professor Charles Finch is in agreement with this view. On page 215 of his book, he says:

> [T]he passage is entirely spurious. These words could never have issued from the pen of a pious Jew such as Josephus; the passage is so transparent a forgery that not even conservative exegetes use it to prove the historicity of Jesus. Thus, Josephus never wrote that paragraph; it was inserted into the text by a later Christian redactor to bolster the case for the historical existence of the Gospel Jesus.

One would have expected other ancient scholars such as Tacitus and Plutarch, who were interested in history and religion, to have mentioned something substantial on JESUS or variations on this name, but are surprisingly silent. Professor John G. Jackson does, however, mention the fact that two Roman sources do mention the name CHRIST or variations on that name: Tacitus and Pliny the Younger. Jackson says:

> Cornelius Tacitus, the Roman historian, in his celebrated *Annals,* refers to the burning of Rome in 64 A.D. and the Neroian persecution of the Christians. He describes them as a "vast multitude" and says that the cult was founded by Christus, who was punished as a criminal by the Procurator Pontius Pilate ... Pliny the Younger, proconsul of Bithynia, wrote a letter to the Roman Emperor Trajan (early second century), in which he reported the presence in his province of a group of people who gathered before daybreak on a certain day and sang hymns to Christ as God. There is no evidence that this Christ was the Jesus of the Gospels.

Many people think the term 'Christ' was the surname of Jesus. This is incorrect. Christ is actually a title and it means 'anointed'. This is why scholars look for the name Jesus in ancient records and not the term Christ. As the historians have found, the only authentic early sources that mention Jesus, or a variation on this name, is the collection of Oral Law compiled by Jewish rabbis called the Talmud. What do these sources say?

The sources, according to Professor Charles Finch, page 209, speak of an individual called Joshua or Jeschu Ben Pandera. Born in around 120 BC to a young woman called Miriam, his father was called Josepth Pantzer or Pandera. There is some speculation that the father could even have been a Roman soldier. In any case, Jeschu Ben Pandera joined a community of Essenes or Therapeutae in Egypt. They lived a communitarian life based on ascetic living, strict cleanliness, prayer, meditation and a vegetarian diet. The Therapeutae possessed remarkable powers of healing. In later years, the young Joshua studied with an Essene teacher called Ben Parachia. In his middle years he left Egypt for Palestine. He taught, healed, and worked "wonders." However, this brought him into conflict with the Jewish authorities who accused him of practising "magic." Consequently they hanged him on the Passover at Lydda in 70 BC. He died aged 50.

Professor Finch adds:

> One tradition states that Jeschu was related to Salome, the queen of King Jannaeus, who protected him during the course of his ministry from the heavy hand of Jewish law. However, she died in 71 B.C., whereupon the sacerdotal enemies of Jeschu speedily seized upon the occasion to judicially do away with him. Thus, the Gospel allusion to the "kingship" of Jesus may have had a tinge of historical truth behind it, since he may have been related to the royal family of Judah."

CHAPTER FOUR: CHRISTIAN BELIEFS AND PRACTICES

Christianity, like earlier religions, divided its followers into the initiates, who were taught esoteric knowledge, and the masses, who were taught exoteric knowledge. There were therefore two groups of people, equally seeing themselves as Christians, but with very different levels of knowledge.

To illustrate this idea, consider the relationship between Christianity and sun worship. For those living north of the equator, the days get progressively longer from winter to summer, with more and more sunlight, and progressively shorter from summer to winter, with less and less sunlight. Halfway between winter to summer, there is the single day where there are exactly 12 hours of day and 12 hours of night. This is the Autumnal Equinox and takes place around the 21 September. Similarly, halfway between summer and winter, there is a single day where there are exactly 12 hours of day and 12 hours of night. This is the Vernal Equinox which takes place around 21 March.

Religions that were based on sun worship traditionally had an important festival just after the shortest day of the year, which is, incidentally, 21 December. The next three days were equally short. However the 25 December was noticeably longer than the previous few days with slightly more sunlight. Sun worshipping religions would celebrate this day as the birth of the new Sun. Professor John G. Jackson quotes Bishop William Montgomery Brown as writing the following in his *Pagan Origins of the Christ Myth:*

> Suppose you had been a child living in Rome 1940 years ago; that is, a few years before Jesus is supposed to have been born. About a week before December twenty-fifth, you would have found everybody preparing for a great feast, just as they do in Europe to-day. To those Romans December twenty-fifth was the birthday of the sun. They wrote that in gold letters in their calendars. Every year about that time, the middle of winter, the sun was born once more and it was going to put an end to the darkness and misery of winter ... Just outside Rome there was an underground temple of the Persian God Mithra. Well, at midnight, the first minute of December twenty-fifth, you would have seen that temple all lit up with candles, and priests in white garments at the altar, and boys burning incense ... Then suppose you asked somebody where

> the Egyptians who lived in Rome had their temple. You would have found these also celebrating the birth of their saviour-god Horus who was born of a virgin in a stable on December twenty-fifth. In the temple you would find a statue or figure of the infant-god Horus lying in a manger, and a statue of his virgin-mother Isis standing beside it ... Then you might go to the Greek temple, and find them paying respect to the figure of their saviour-god in a manger or cradle. And if you found the quarters of the gladiators, the war-captives from Germany, you would have found these also holding a feast, and they would explain that December twenty-fifth (or mid-winter) was, all over Europe, the great feast of Yule.

As the days start to get longer from the end of December through January, there was always the worry that day may not eventually conquer night. Consequently, the birth of the sun and his growth was considered perilous. This is why many religions have the idea that the sun is at risk of being killed by an evil enemy soon after its birth. In the Christian story, the young Jesus is threatened by King Herod.

Eventually, we get to the Vernal Equinox where day and night is of equal length. After this period, day definitely conquers night. Consequently, sun worshipping religions have the idea that their deity conquers death at this point of the year. In the Christian story, Jesus dies, resurrects and ascends to heaven during this period. To demonstrate that Easter really is an astronomical festival and not a real earthly event, why does Easter shift every year? If it commemorates the death and resurrection of the Christian deity, no one can die and resurrect on different days of each year. So what is going on here?

Easter is calculated as the first full moon after the Vernal Equinox. The Christians then celebrate the Friday and the Sunday after this full moon. This is why it shifts every year. It is not an earthly celebration, it is an astronomical celebration. Christian initiates always understood this. The masses are generally unaware of this information.

According to Gerald Massey, the mummified and anointed body of Osiris was called the Karast. Other Egyptologists claim that the word Karast means burial. In Christianity, Jesus does not become the Christ until he has been anointed. The New Testament is a Greek language document and the word Christ was originally Kristos and means anointed. It is therefore very likely that there is a connection between the Egyptian Karast and Greek Kristos.

The Ancient Egyptian deity, Osiris, was associated with corn and also with grapes. The products associated with corn and grapes are bread and wine. There is clearly a relationship between this and the Christian Eucharist.

Figure 12. Our Lady of Anjony, Castle of Anjony, France, seventeenth century. This is one of 450-plus such images in Europe.

According to Reverend Charles H. Vail, there is a connection between an Ancient Egyptian festival and Lent: "The Osiris of Egypt was supposed to be dead or absent forty days in each year during which the people lamented his loss as the Syrians did that of Adonis."

The Christians continue to end their prayers with Amen. Like the Jews, Christians claim that Amen means so be it. As stated earlier, Amen, also written as Amun, was the chief deity of the ancient Egyptian city of Waset (also known as Thebes) and the chief deity of the Kushite city of Jebel Barkal.

Catholic and Orthodox Christians continue to venerate the mother goddess. The Ancient Egyptian and Sudanese deity Isis was the virgin mother to Horus. She was associated with the harvest, and with the constellation Virgo. Every new pharaoh of Egypt claimed to be reborn as the son of Isis (i.e. as the new Horus). Professor Danita Redd has shown that many of the early icons of Mary and Jesus in European Christendom are shown as Black. Among these are Our Lady of Montserrat (in Spain), The Queen of the Pyrenees (in Spain), Our Lady of the Hermits (in Switzerland) and Our Lady of Czestochowa (in Poland). I am of the belief that since many of these icons wear veils, this may well reflect the influence of the goddess Neith.

Finally, Professor Charles Finch shows the direct link between the Ancient Egyptian belief system and Christianity. During the period when the Romans conquered Egypt, many people worshipped Serapis, a deity that combined aspects of Osiris and Hapi. Hapi is the deity associated with the Nile river. On the Denderah Zodiac, he is shown as the water carrier, the prototype of Aquarius. Professor Charles Finch quotes from a letter on page 215 written by the Emperor Hadrian which reads as follows: "Those who worship Serapis likewise are Christians, even those who style themselves Bishops of Christ are devoted to Serapis." This shows that in the evolution of religious belief from the Ancient Egyptian worship of Osiris to Christianity, believers adored an intermediate deity called Serapis. Serapis worshippers called themselves Christians. Therefore, it is highly likely that when the Roman sources, Tacitus and Pliny the Younger, mentioned Christians, it was the Serapis worshippers that they were referring to.

CHAPTER FIVE: THE RIGHT WING COUNTERATTACK

Over the last few years, a literature has developed in the United States coming from the far Christian Right. Publishing houses like Huntingdon Press have popularised a literature that seeks to defend Christianity against Masonic and Luciferian influences. What they mean by these terms is broad. Lucifer means 'light bringer'. It is also a name for the Devil in Christianity. It is also related to 'illuminated' meaning enlightened, and thus to 'illuminati'. Some argue that Masons secretly practise an Ecumenical religion that draws from Pagan influences (i.e. from Ancient Egypt, Canaan and Babylonia) but publicly pretend to be Christians. Others accuse Masonic scholarship (such as Reverend Charles H. Vail and Albert Churchward), of exaggerating Pagan influences on Christianity in order to undermine Christianity. Some of the writers and popularisers would make Luciferian an equivalent word to Satanic. This same literature warns against the New World Order and its coming anti-Christian religion.

This right wing literature insists that Jesus is the Only Way to God, the Truth and the Light. There are no other ways and therefore Christianity should not compromise with any other belief system. Many such writers would even denounce a book, such as this, as being influenced by Luciferianism.

There is, however, a serious problem with this approach. We have already seen that the Nativity of Jesus is undoubtedly a copy of earlier religious traditions. We have seen that the Life of Jesus has many episodes copied from earlier religious traditions. We have seen that Christmas and Easter have elements copied from earlier religious traditions. We have seen that the Eucharist is heavily influenced by earlier religious traditions. We have seen that the original Madonna and Child were in fact Isis and Horus. Moreover, the veiled Madonna was influenced by the Goddess Neith. Finally we have seen that Christianity continues to end its prayers by naming an Ancient Egyptian and Sudanese deity, Amen.

There is more. Acts 7:22 claims that Moses was learned in all the wisdom of the Egyptians. Since tradition claims that Moses wrote the first five books of the Bible (also called the Torah and the Pentateuch) then the first five books of the Bible must contain influences that right-wing Christians would have to consider Luciferian.

Proverbs Chapters 22 and 23 contain portions that are word-for-word copies of an Ancient Egyptian text. Since tradition claims that Solomon wrote Proverbs. He too must have been under the influence of Luciferianism.

Psalms Chapter 104 also contains portions that are almost word-for-word copies of an Ancient Egyptian text. Since tradition claims that David wrote this. He too must have been under the influence of Luciferianism.

The Reverend Charles H. Vail tells us that Christian ceremonies such as the Fasts are of pre-Christian origin, Baptism is of pre-Christian origin, and the Eucharist or Communion is of pre-Christian origin. Therefore, if the right-wing Christians are correct, anyone who practices these things must be influenced by Luciferianism also. Or is it that the Reverend Vail is lying because he was a Mason? Whichever be the case, plenty of non-Masonic scholars say similar things to Vail. Professor Beckford, for example, asked the Egyptologist Dr Bojana Mojsov: "Which other elements within this [Egyptian] passion play, within this myth, have parallels with Christianity?" Dr Mojsov replied:

> Well, baptism in the holy river in the Nile which was considered to be a sacred river. The sacred Nile water which was carried into the temple and the statues were anointed with it ... The eating of corn bread as the body of Osiris because corn came about through the sacrifice of Osiris.

It should be clear to most readers, that once the Jesus story is removed from Christianity, once suspicion is thrown over Moses, Solomon and David, there isn't a great deal left that is untouched by what the right wing would call Luciferian influence. The only thing left is the historical Jesus or Jeschu Ben Pandera. Even he studied in Egypt.

For the record, I do not agree that pointing out similarities between Christianity and pre-Christian religions makes one a Luciferian or a Satanist. I am of the opinion that religious believers should learn as much as they can about their religion and religion in general and use that knowledge to improve their religious practice. Can I get an Amen to that?

BIBLIOGRAPHY

Francisco Alvarez is quoted in Graham Hancock, *The Beauty of Historic Ethiopia,* Kenya, Camerapix, 1996, p.39

Robert Beckford, *The Hidden Story of Jesus* (documentary), UK, Juniper Communications, 2007

E. A. Wallis Budge, *A History of Ethiopia, Nubia & Abyssinia,* Volume 1, UK, Methuen & Co., pp.156-159

John Henrik Clarke, *A Great and Mighty Walk* (documentary), US, Black Dot Media, 1996

J. C. deGraft-Johnson, *African Glory,* UK, Watts & Co., 1954, pp.32, 37-52

Nnamdi Elleh, *African Architecture: Evolution and Transformation,* US, McGraw-Hill, 1997, p.41

Mrs Stuart Erskine, *Vanished Cities of Northern Africa,* UK, Hutchinson & Co., no date given for publication, p.81

Charles S. Finch, *Echoes of the Old Darkland,* US, Khenti, 1991, pp.209, 215, also 179-216

Peter Garlake, *Early Art and Architecture of Africa,* UK, Oxford University Press, 2002, p.73

Georg Gerster, *Churches in Rock,* London, Phaidon, 1970, p.62

Joseph E. Harris ed., *Pillars in Ethiopian History: The William Leo Hansberry African History Notebook, Volume 1,* US, Howard University Press, 1974, pp.64-70

Godfrey Higgins, *Anacalypsis, Volumes I* and *II,* UK, Longman, Rees, Orme, Brown & Green, 1836

John G. Jackson, *Christianity Before Christ,* US, American Atheist Press, 1985, p.1

John G. Jackson, *Pagan Origins of the Christ Myth,* US, American Atheist Press, 1988, pp.7, 8, 11-12

Martin Luther King Jr., *A Study of Mithraism,* 1949, see https://kinginstitute.stanford.edu/king-papers/documents/study-mithraism

Gerald Massey, *Ancient Egypt: The Light of the World, Volume 2,* UK, T. Fisher Unwin, 1907, pp.690-914

Anu M'Bantu & Fari Supiya, *Ethiopia's First Christian Emperor: Ezana of Axum,* in *West Africa,* Issue 4303, UK, Afrimedia International, 26 November - 2 December 2001, p.43

Runoko Rashidi, *Uncovering the African Past,* UK, Books of Africa, 2015, pp.131-135

Danita Redd, *Black Madonnas of Europe,* in *Black Women in Antiquity,* ed Ivan Van Sertima, US, Transaction Publishers, 1988, pp.162-187

J. A. Rogers, *Sex and Race: Volume I,* US, Helga M. Rogers, 1968, p.282

Edward Scobie, *African Popes,* in *African Presence in Early Europe,* ed Ivan Van Sertima, US, Transaction Publishers, 1985, pp.96-107

Charles H. Vail, *The World's Saviours,* UK, Fowler, 1913, pp.138, 137-155

Robin Walker, *When We Ruled: Second Edition,* UK, Reklaw Education, 2013, pp.559-591

Larry Williams & Charles S. Finch, *The Great Queens of Ethiopia,* in *Black Women in Antiquity,* ed Ivan Van Sertima, US, Transaction Publishers, 1988, pp.20-33

PART THREE

BLACK INFLUENCES IN THE ORIGIN OF ISLAM AND THE INDIAN RELIGIONS

INTRODUCTION

Caliph Umar's powerful influence in the history of Islam has led writers to call him 'the Saint Paul of Islam.' The first Caliph of the East after Abu Bekr, he was a Companion of the Prophet and the founder of the Umayyad Dynasty. He spoke very highly of an African Companion of the Prophet called Bilal and described him as the "third part of Islam." What does this mean? Who is Bilal? What do we know about Bilal?

There is a pseudo problem with the origin of Islam. In the Semitic languages, S-L-M means peace. Adding vowels, S-L-M becomes 'Shalom' in Hebrew and is a greeting that means peace (and also prosperity). 'Salaam' is the Arabic equivalent and means peace. Notice that both words, Shalom and Salaam, have S as a first letter, L as a middle letter and M as a last letter. In Arabic, MU denotes a person. Therefore a 'Muslim' (i.e. MU + SLM) is one who has peace within himself from his submission to Al'lah. Moreover, 'Islam' implies the attainment of peace through submission to Al'lah. Using this definition, Muslims claim that Islam is actually the world's first religion. For example, Sura 2:136 reads: "Say Ye: 'We believe in Allah and the revelation given to us, and to Abraham, Isma'il, Isaac, Jacob and the Tribes, and that given to Moses and Jesus, and that given to (all) Prophets from their Lord: We make no difference between one and another of them: and we submit to Allah.'" Believing that Adam and Eve were the first two people on earth, Islam claims that they were Muslims also because they achieved peace through their submission to Al'lah.

In this essay, I shall avoid chronologically impossible claims about Islam being the world's first religion. Similarly, Christians cannot be allowed to get away with a theology that claims that when Genesis 1:26 says: "and God said, let us make man in our image, after our likeness", that God the Father was talking to God the Son. Therefore, I assert that Islam could only begin during the time of the Prophet Muhammad given as 571 to 632 CE.

Islam was built on four main ideas: Judaism, Christianity, rejection of St Paul's teachings, and Pan-Arabism.

The oldest of these ideas was Judaism. As with Christianity, Islam is another religion that attempts to bring Judaism to the masses. Islam accepts the writings associated with Moses (the Torah or Pentateuch), David (the Psalms), and Solomon (the Proverbs).

Secondly, Islam was built on Christianity. Muslims accept the writings about the Prophet Jesus (the Gospels). For example, the Gospel of John 14:16 says: "and I will pray the Father, and he shall give you another Comforter, that he may abide with you for ever." Muslims interpret this passage as a prophecy made by Jesus that refers to Muhammad. Of all the Gospels, however, Muslims prefer the Gospel of Barnabas, which is often sold by itself in Islamic bookshops.

Thirdly, Islam was built on a rejection of anything or any texts to do with or inspired by St Paul. Islam teaches that Jesus, like all the prophets, called on his followers to worship God Almighty only. He did not call on his followers to worship him. It was St Paul who popularised the worship of Jesus.

Fourthly, Islam was built on Pan-Arabism. Unlike Christianity, where there is no longer an ecclesiastical language and Bibles can be authorised to be used in churches in any language, this cannot be done with the Qur'an. It can only be an Arabic language document. It is therefore expected that Muslims will learn Arabic in order to read the Qur'an. Moreover, the names of the individuals in the Qur'an have all been Arabicised. Consequently, Abraham became Ibrahim, Moses became Musa, Joseph became Yusuf, Enoch became Idris, etcetera. In keeping with the Pan-Arab agenda, the holiest cities of Islam are both in Arabia. A good Muslim is expected to do hajj (or pilgrimage) to those cities at least once in their lifetime.

CHAPTER ONE: A HISTORICAL SKETCH OF ISLAM

According to Professor J. C. deGraft-Johnson, the Prophet was born in 571 CE (others say 570 CE). His name, Muhammad, means the Praiser. He was of the Quraish tribe of western Arabia and married a wealthy widow of a rich merchant in Mecca. During this period, Mecca was the centre for the worship of the Goddess Al'lat through her symbol, the meteorite, Al Ka'aba.

Professor Cheikh Anta Diop says that during this period: "Yemen was a Negro Ethiopian colony and remained so until the birth of Mohammed." Why is this of significance? A web page called *Islamic Architecture History* contains the following information:

> In 630C.E. Muhammad's army reconquered the city of Mecca from the Banu Quraish tribe. The holy sanctuary of Ka'ba was rebuilt and re-dedicated to Islam, the reconstruction being carried out before Muhammad's death in 632C.E. by a shipwrecked Abyssinian carpenter in his native style. This sanctuary was amongst the first major works of Islamic architecture. The walls were decorated with paintings of Jesus, Mary, Abraham, prophets, angels and trees. Later doctrines of Islam dating from the eighth century and originating from the Hadith, forbade the use of such icons in architecture, specifically those of humans and animals.

However, Peter Garlake, an authority on African art and architecture gives a different date. He states that: "It is probable that the Ka'aba of Mecca, rebuilt in 609, is, behind its veils, a classic Aksumite building."

In around the year 611 CE, when Muhammad was around 40 years old (others say 30 years old), he began to develop prophetic leanings. Apparently the Angel Gabriel (or Jibrail) communicated religious verses in rhyming couplets to him which would ultimately become the Qur'an. Muhammad spoke to his wife about his revelations, and later preached to his servants and close associates. These became his first disciples. Bilal, an Ethiopian, was one of the early converts. However, since the majority of Muslims believe that Islam is the world's first religion, most prefer to call converts 'reverts' instead.

In around 615, the Prophet (or some say his followers) spent time in Ethiopia under Emperor Armah. Armah offered sanctuary to some of the

Figure 13. Coin of Emperor Armah of Ethiopia.

first converts to the new religion fleeing from persecution in Arabia. Dr Rashidi thinks this probably explains why the Prophet said: "Who brings an Ethiopian man or an Ethiopian woman into his house, brings the blessing of God there."

Dawud Walid on a web page entitled 7 *Luminous Black Companions of the Prophet,* names Black Arabs and Ethiopians who were intimately connected with the life of the Prophet. Adib Rashad mentions others on his 2005 article entitled *African Contributions to the Rise of Islam.*

Among these were Barakah, also known as Umm Ayman, was an Abyssinian servant and wet-nurse who helped to raise the young Muhammad. Usamah bin Zayd was an adopted son of the Prophet who the Prophet elected as General to command a battle against the Romans in Syria. Mihja' bin Salih was one of the early adherents of Islam in Mecca. Incidentally, Dr Runoko Rashidi mentions a tradition that claims he was the very first Muslim ever to be killed in battle. Ammar bin Yasir was one of the Companions of the Prophet who migrated to Abyssinia finding protection under Armah. Two of the Prophet's wives were Africans, Umm Habiba and Maryam, an Egyptian Copt. Finally, Julaybib was one of the early martyrs of Islam. The Prophet personally dug his grave and interred him.

In 628 the Prophet sent letters and envoys to Emperor Heraclitus of Byzantium, King Kavadh of Persia, and Emperor Tai-tsung of China demanding that they convert to the worship of the one true God, where Muhammad was the prophet. The Persian king destroyed the letter and sent the messengers away. The Chinese ruler received the messengers well and even allowed them to build the Canton Mosque--the oldest such building in the world.

In 629 CE the Prophet and his followers took control of Mecca (others give different dates). This became the holiest city in Islam and Medina became the second key city. The Prophet died three years later and Abu Bekr became the First Caliph. During this period, the Arabs conquered far and wide. Between 639 CE and 708 CE, the Arabs had conquered their way across the whole of North Africa. They spread Islam into Africa, but they also ended most of the early Christian heritage there. They also displaced the indigenous North Africans and pushed these populations further south into Africa. This is why Black people are concentrated in Africa 'south of the Sahara.'

CHAPTER TWO: BILAL IBN RAHAB

Bilal ibn Rabah is one of the most interesting and controversial characters in Black history. What we know about him remains controversial indeed.

Mainstream scholarship uses his life and achievements as a political football to suit racist ideologies that cannot be supported historically. For example, Wikipedia says "racism and sociopolitical [status] of Arabia prevented Bilal from achieving a lofty position in society." In the same article we read: "the Quraysh despised Bilal and called him ibn Sauda (son of the black woman)." These claims are not credible. It gives the impression that Black people, specifically from Ethiopia, enjoyed low status in Arabia when this cannot possibly have been true. Saudi Arabian racism against foreigners in contemporary times, specifically Black foreigners, is becoming more and more apparent to the outside world. However, what may be true of the world of today, has no bearing on the time period that we are speaking of i.e. the sixth and seventh centuries CE.

To illustrate this point, Edward Gibbon, the great English historian and author of *The Decline and Fall of the Roman Empire* wrote the following in Chapter 50:

> Mahomet ... sprung from the tribe of Koreish and the family of Hashem, the most illustrious of the Arabs, the princes of Mecca, and the hereditary guardians of the Caaba. The grandfather of Mahomet was Abdol Motalleb, the son of Hashem, a wealthy and generous citizen, who relieved the distress of famine with the supplies of commerce. Mecca, which had been fed by the liberality of the father, was saved by the courage of the son. The kingdom of Yemen was subject to the Christian princes of Abyssinia; their vassal Abrahah was provoked by an insult to avenge the honour of the cross; and the holy city was invested by a train of elephants and an army of Africans. A treaty was proposed; and, in the first audience, the grandfather of Mahomet demanded the restitution of his cattle. "And why," said Abrahah, "do you not rather implore my clemency in favour of your temple, which I have threatened to destroy?" "Because," replied the intrepid chief, "the cattle is my own; the Caaba belongs to the gods, and they will defend their house from injury and sacrilege." The want of provisions, or the valour of the Koreish, compelled the Abyssinians to a disgraceful retreat: their discomfiture has been adorned with a miraculous flight of birds, who showered down stones on the heads of the infidels; and the

> deliverance was long commemorated by the era of the elephant. The glory of Abdol Motalleb was crowned with domestic happiness; his life was prolonged to the age of one hundred and ten years; and he became the father of six daughters and thirteen sons. His best beloved Abdallah was the most beautiful and modest of the Arabian youth; and in the first night, when he consummated his marriage with Amina, of the noble race of the Zahrites, two hundred virgins are said to have expired of jealousy and despair. Mahomet, or more properly Mohammed, the only son of Abdallah and Amina, was born at Mecca, four years after the death of Justinian, and two months after the defeat of the Abyssinians, whose victory would have introduced into the Caaba the religion of the Christians.

Edward Gibbon is correct, the Ethiopians or Abyssinians were, at one time, the rulers of Yemen. Had they enjoyed even more military success, the Ka'aba of Mecca would indeed have become a centre of Christianity. Therefore all claims that Bilal enjoyed low status because he was Black and from Abyssinia, when THE ABYSSINIANS WERE AT ONE TIME THE RULING POWER IN THE REGION must be dismissed as utter nonsense and brings severe discredit against those who would repeat such obvious nonsense.

At the beginning of this essay, I cited Caliph Umar saying that Bilal was the "third part of Islam." Professor Yosef ben-Jochannan in *African Origins of the Major 'Western' Religions* incorrectly interpreted this to mean that Al'lah was the first part of Islam, and the Prophet was the second part. The rest of his essay was uncritically based on a biographical sketch of Bilal by the great Jamaican historian, J. A. Rogers. However, the Rogers essay is radically at odds with nearly all mainstream Islamic teaching. Moreover, the content of the essay is unsupported by the bibliography given by Rogers. I shall therefore pass the ben-Jochannan/Rogers data concerning Bilal in silence.

Helmi Sharawi, an Egyptian Africanist, in a book called *Imagining the Arab Other: How Arabs and Non-Arabs Represent Each Other,* edited by Tahar Labib, presents the Umar quote as "He is equal to one third of Muslims." Unfortunately Sharawi makes no comment on what this idea may mean. The original source of the Umar quote was Al Jahiz who wrote: "Also among the blacks was: the Ethiopian, Bilal, of whom Caliph Omar said that he alone was worth a third of all Islam." However this is to be interpreted, Caliph Umar's statement still represents very high praise for Bilal. In a similar vein, Rashidi quotes the Prophet as saying the following to Bilal: "As I journeyed in paradise and was mounting the stairs of God I heard your footsteps before me."

Figure 14. Islamic miniature from sixteenth century Turkey depicting Bilal giving the Call to Prayer in Mecca. Notice that most of the Muslims, except Bilal, have been given Mongolian features typical of early Turkish people. Because of the pale complexions used in Turkish art, White scholars freely reproduce this material to create the same anti-Black propaganda effect that the bogus Mary and Jesus imagery has in Christianity.

Wikipedia says that Bilal ibn Rabah was born in the year 580 AD. His father Rabah was a slave while his mother, Hamamah, was a former Abyssinian princess who was captured and enslaved after an attempt to destroy the Ka'aba. However, other sources challenge both the date of his birth and the birth place. One website, http://www.alahazrat.net, claims: "His birth place is Abyssinia (Ethiopia) and this is why he is known as Habshi (the old name for Abyssinia is Habsh). Born in the late 6th century, the preferred view is that Bilal Radi Allahu Ta'ala Anhu was 43 years old at the time of Hijra but it has been suggested by some that he could have been as old as 53." If true, this means he could even have been born as early as 569 AD.

Wikipedia narrates that Bilal followed his parents into slavery. His enslaver was Umayyah ibn Khalaf. However, through hard work, Bilal became recognised as a good slave and was even entrusted with the keys to the Idols of Arabia. However, when Muhammad announced his prophethood, Bilal was attracted to his message and was amongst his earliest converts. Bilal renounced idol worship and as a result was subjected to increasingly violent torture by his enslaver. However, Bilal refused to renounce his new faith.

News of Bilal's resolve reached some of the Companions of the Prophet who informed Muhammad. Muhammad sent Abu Bakr to negotiate a deal with Umayyah to purchase Bilal and emancipate him from slavery. However, http://www.alahazrat.net, tell a very different story:

> Hadrat Abu Bakr then approached the Jew while he was again torturing Hadrat Bilal. Hadrat Abu Bakr said to him, "Why are you beating this friend of Allah?" How long will you carry out this practice on this poor person?" Umayyah bin Khalaf retorted that, 'since you have instigated him (by teaching Islam to him) so you free him." Hadrat Abu Bakr Radi Allahu Ta'ala Anhu answered, "Yes, I will free him. I have a black slave who is even stronger than him and who is in your religion. Will you accept this slave in exchange for him?" Umayyah bin Khalaf accepted the offer.

In 622 AD Bilal, along with the other Muslims, migrated to Yathrib or Medina. Over the next decade, Bilal accompanied Muhammad on all his military expeditions. After Medina emerged as a well established Islamic state, the Prophet appointed Bilal as the Secretary of Treasure for Medina. This was a most prominent position. Controlling the entire budget, Bilal distributed funds to widows, orphans, travellers, and people who could not support themselves.

According to Wikipedia, both Sunnis and Shia Muslims agree that the *Adhan* (call to prayer) was established by Muhammad in approximately

622 or 623 AD. He chose Bilal to be the first muezzin (i.e. person who would perform the Call to Prayer) because of his deep, melodious, and resonant voice. Although Sunnis and Shias have slightly different versions of how the *Adhan* was established, both agree that Bilal was the first muezzin in Islam.

The lines of the *Adhan* sung by Bilal were:

> Allah is the greatest, Allah is the greatest.
> I acknowledge that there is no deity but God.
> I acknowledge that Muhammad is the Messenger of Allah.
> Hasten to prayer.
> Hasten to success.
> Prayer is better than sleep.
> Allah is greatest.
> There is no deity but God.

Wikipedia narrates that Bilal participated in the Battle of Badr, the Battle of Uhud, the Battle of the Trench, and in all of the major events in the early phase of Islam. In January 630 CE, the Muslims took control of Mecca through nonviolent means. After the capture, Bilal ascended to the top of the Ka'aba and called the believers to prayer. It was the first time the Call to Prayer was performed in Mecca.

After the death of the Prophet, Sunni scholars say that Bilal accompanied the Muslim armies, under the command of Said ibn Aamir al-Jumahi, to Syria. Bilal never performed the Call to Prayer again. However, when Caliph Umar visited Jerusalem, the Companions of the Prophet requested Umar to ask Bilal for one last *Adhan* which was granted. When Bilal called the *Adhan,* all of the Companions were overcome by emotion remembering Muhammad.

Shia scholars, however, tell a very different tale. They say that Bilal refused to give an oath of allegiance to Abu Bakr following the death of the Prophet. Moreover, they claim he even wrote a poem that underlines this lack of allegiance:

> By Allah! I did not turn towards Abu Bakr,
> If Allah had not protected me,
> hyena would have stood on my limbs.
> Allah has bestowed on me good
> and honoured me,
> Surely there is vast good with Allah.
> You will not find me following an innovator,
> Because I am not an innovator, as they are.

Figure 15. Shrine of Bilal in Rabahiya, Amman in Jordan, Photo: بلال الدويك

A consequence of this, Bilal was exiled from Medina by both Umar and by Abu Bakr. He migrated to Syria and became one of the earliest Shias.

Wikipedia says Sunni and Shia scholars are agreed that Bilal died in Damascus at some point between 638 and 642 CE. Some say he was 63 years old when he died. However, the information presented by http://www.alahazrat.net may indicate that he could have died at the age of 73. Wikipedia suggest that Bilal is probably buried in the Bab al-Saghir cemetery in Damascus, Syria. Moreover, there is a shrine built in Bilal's honour in a village called Rabahiya on the outskirts of Amman, Jordan.

Islamic Guidance have a website with sermons about the important personalities in Islam. The sermon on Bilal ends with the following idea:

> Do you know what the inheritance of Bilal was? It was the *Adhan*. From generation to generation, the Muslims have adopted the *Adhan,* and this is the 'Sunnah' of Bilal RA. From Australia to Canada, from China to Argentina, from Mauritius to Iceland, a million times a day the *Adhan* is given, a million times a day the 'Sunnah' of Bilal is revived.

CHAPTER THREE: ON THE ETHNICITY OF THE PROPHET

Scholars generally accept that Abd al-Muttalib was the grandfather of the Prophet. David Samuel Margoliouth, then Professor of Arabic at the University of Oxford wrote a classic text called *Mohammed and the Rise of Islam* in 1905. Wikipedia confirms that "his works on the history of Islam became the standard treatises in English". Professor Margoliouth wrote the following about the Prophet's grandfather in this book:

> Abd alMuttalib, "slave of al-Muttalib," of which a fanciful explanation is given by our historians, is probably to be interpreted as meaning that its owner was at one time actually a slave, though afterwards manumitted and enrolled in the Hashim clan. The names of his ten sons and six daughters are probably historical, and indeed four of the former and two of the latter play parts of importance in the sequel. All ten sons, it is said, were of massive build and dark colour.

The ten sons included the Prophet's father and his brothers. How dark were they? How dark is dark? Professor Margoliouth gives his primary source for this information as "Jahiz, Opuscula, 75, 5." This was a collection of Al Jahiz's works that Gerlof van Vloten edited and translated. J. A. Rogers in *World's Great Men of Color, Volume 1,* quotes directly from Al Jahiz. Moreover, Professor Vincent J. Cornell, a European American expert on Arabic, produced a newer and fresh translation of Al Jahiz more recently. Rogers quotes the passage as: "The ten sons of Abd el Mottalib were all black and strong." Vincent J Cornell translates the same passage on page 50 of his book as: "Abd al-Muttalib father ten Lords, Black as the night and magnificent."

Professor Ivan Van Sertima has urged scholars not to jump to hasty conclusions because of this evidence. Arabic families were traditionally polygamous and if one does not know the ethnicity of the mother, one should not make unwarranted conclusions. However, it is common in Islamic circles to do just that and make unwarranted conclusions. Some Muslims assert that the Prophet of Islam was White based on Hadith passages where the Prophet is described as 'abyad' (i.e. white). Is this conclusive? *The Encyclopedia of Islam, Volume V,* page 705 explains:

> One of the most striking manifestations of the symbolic connotations of colours among the Arabs, is the phenomenon of opposites ... We have seen, in studying the semantic value of certain adjectives of colour, that they were sometimes capable of embracing two diametrically opposite meanings. This phenomenon is particularly to be noted in the case of white and black.

Consequently, the term 'abyad' is not always the anti-Black trump card that many Muslims think it is.

Just before the death of the Prophet, he gave a powerful speech at Mecca known as the *Farewell Sermon.* Scholars are not agreed on what he said but two quoted passages are worthy of discussion. The online Islamic Encyclopedia quotes the Prophet as saying: "O People! Listen and obey, though a mangled Abyssinian slave be your Amir, so long as he executes (the ordinance of) the Book of Allah among you." Another website, History for the Relaxed Historian, quotes the passage as: "O people! Though an Abyssinian slave may become your amir [ruler], listen and obey him, as long as he executes the Book of Allah among you." This strongly supports the Rogers/ben-Jochannan idea that the Prophet initially offered the position of Caliph to Bilal.

The second key passage is: "an Arab has no superiority over a non-Arab nor a non-Arab has any superiority over an Arab; also a white has no superiority over black nor a black has any superiority over white". One website, Islamo-Criticism, has doubted the authenticity of the passage. Significantly, this passage is NOT included in the online Islamic Encyclopedia or the History for the Relaxed Historian versions of the sermon. I also doubt the authenticity of the passage. I believe that ideologues inserted it to deviously insinuate that the Prophet was White. A Black prophet would have reversed the second half of the passage. Thus a Black prophet would have said: "a black has no superiority over white nor a white has any superiority over black".

CHAPTER FOUR: ISLAM IN AFRICAN HISTORY: AN INTRODUCTION

Islam has had a big impact in African history, positive and negative. In *When We Ruled,* I describe the civilisation of the Moors of Northwest Africa and Spain in Chapter 13. I describe the West and Central African superstates: Ancient Ghana, Mediaeval Mali, the Songhai Empire and the Kanem Borno Empire in Chapters 12 and 14. In addition, I describe the Hausa Confederation of Northern Nigeria and the Swahili Confederation of the East African coast in Chapters 14 and 15.

In the mean time being, I will introduce two African personalities who are important in the history of Islam: Dhu l-Nun al-Misri and Mansa Musa I.

Dhu l-Nun al-Misri is considered the founder of Sufi Islam. Born in Upper Egypt in 796 CE, and of a light complexion, he is considered the first to enunciate the Sufi concepts of ecstatic states and the mystic ways towards the true knowledge of God. He died in 859 CE. His tomb is preserved in Cairo. Wikipedia quotes an incident in his life from a mediaeval source:

> A story from the life of the ninth-century Sufi, Dhu-l-Nun, the Egyptian, illustrates this: I was wandering in the mountains when I observed a party of afflicted folk gathered together. "What befell you?" I asked. "There is a devotee living in a cell here," they answered. "Once every year he comes out and breathes on these people and they are all healed. Then he returns to his cell, and does not emerge again until the following year." I waited patiently until he came out. I beheld a man pale of cheek, wasted and with sunken eyes. The awe of him caused me to tremble. He looked on the multitude with compassion. Then he raised his eyes to heaven, and breathed several times over the afflicted ones. All were healed. As he was about to retire to his cell, I seized his skirt. "For the love of God," I cried. "You have healed the outward sickness; pray heal the inward sickness." "Dhu-l-Nun," he said, gazing at me, "take your hand off me. The Friend is watching from the zenith of might and majesty. If He sees you clutching at another than He, He will abandon you to that person, and that person to you, and you will perish each at the other's hand." So saying, he withdrew into his cell.

Mansa Musa I, the great ruler of Mali, led the greatest Hajj in Islamic history. Professor deGraft-Johnson narrates:

It was in 1324 … that the world awoke to the splendour and grandeur of Mali. There across the African desert, and making its way to Mecca, was a caravan of a size which had never before been seen, a caravan consisting of 60,000 men. They were Mansa Musa's men, and Mansa Musa was with them. He was not going to war: he was merely going to worship at Mecca. The huge caravan included a personal retinue of 12,000 slaves, all dressed in brocade and Persian silk. Mansa Musa himself rode on horseback, and directly preceding him were 500 slaves, each carrying a staff of gold weighing about six pounds (500 mitkal). Then came Mansa Musa's baggage-train of eighty camels, each carrying 300 pounds (three kantar) weight of gold dust. This imposing caravan made its way from Niani on the Upper Niger to Walata, then to Tuat, and then on to Cairo. Mansa Musa's piety and open-handed generosity, the fine clothes and good behaviour of his followers, all quickly made a good impression. One might have thought that a pilgrimage to Mecca undertaken with such pomp and ceremony would have ulterior political motives, but no such motives have ever been adduced.

CHAPTER FIVE: INDUS VALLEY AND THE BIRTH OF SHAIVISM

A very ancient civilisation flourished in the Indus Valley region of Pakistan and Western India. This civilisation was invaded and conquered between 2000 and 1500 BC. The conquerors called themselves Aryans (i.e. 'Nobles'). S. G. Blaxland-Stubbs wrote an instructive essay where he explains what happened next:

> The early Aryan literature of India, the hymns of the Rigveda, which, it is commonly agreed, date from about 1000 B.C., speak of the people whom the proud Aryan invaders found in India as black skinned barbarians ... But Aryan pride of race has received something of a shock from archaeological investigations carried out by Sir John Marshall and, more recently, by Dr E. Mackay in the valley of the Indus. Here ample evidence has been found of a race whose complex civilization and high culture were equal, and in some respects superior, to those of early Mesopotamia and Egypt.

What did they find in the region that caused such a shock to Aryan pride? Professor John G. Jackson, in his masterly *Man, God, and Civilization,* explains what the archaeologists found evidence of:

> The first great civilization of India was established by the Dravidians in the Indus Valley. They built large cities, the principal ones being Mohenjo Daro, Chanhu Daro, and Harappa. These cities were well constructed. Mohenjo Daro was two square miles in area, with regularly laid-out main and side streets, lined with attractive two-story brick houses. Bathrooms were a common feature, and they were fitted out with runaway drains leading to brick sewers laid under the streets. This culture reached its peak about 3000 B.C.

Mr Blaxland-Stubbs informed us that the Aryan literature claims the original inhabitants of India and Pakistan were Black skinned people. Can we substantiate this?

Godfrey Higgins, author of the erudite *Anacalypsis* of 1836, presents evidence relevant to this discussion:

> Mr. Wilsford, in his treatise on Egypt and the Nile, in the Asiatic Researches, informs us, that many very ancient statues of the God Buddha in India have crisp, curly hair, with flat noses and thick lips; and adds, "nor can it be

> reasonably doubted, that a race of Negroes formerly had power and pre-eminence in India." This is confirmed by Mr. Maurice, who says, "The figures in the Hindoo caverns are of a very different character from the present race of Hindoos: their countenances are broad and full, the nose flat, and the lips, particularly the under lip, remarkably thick." This is again confirmed by Colonel Fitzclarence in the journal of his journey from India. And Maurice, in the first volume of his Indian Antiquities, states, that the figures in the caves in India and in the temples in Egypt, are absolutely the same as given by Bruce, Niebuhr, &c.

V. T. Rajshekar, an Indian scholar, presented similar ideas, but much more recently:

> The original inhabitants of India were dark-skinned and closely resembled the Africans in physical features. They founded the Indus Valley Civilization which, according to historians, was one of the world's first and most glorious. Aryan tribes invaded India, destroyed the Indus Valley Civilization, and employed a cunning, deceptive religious ideology to enslave the indigenous people. Those who fled to India's forests and hills later came to be called "tribals." As these native Indians were gradually overcome, captured and enslaved they were kept outside village limits and "untouchability" was enforced upon them ... The native people of India (currently known as "Untouchables, Tribals and Backward Castes") were not Hindus. They were Animists--Nature Worshippers. Since India's Dalits were once autonomous tribal groups, each group was known by its own tribal name. The Aryans created "caste" out of these tribal divisions by hierarchically arranging them in ascending degrees of reverence and descending degrees of contempt ... Aryans based their whole philosophy on color (varna). The four-fold caste system is based on skin (varna) color. The natives are dark-skinned and the Aryans light.

Rajshekar is clear that Hinduism was not the original religion of the India or Pakistan regions. He identifies Hinduism as the religion brought there by the Aryan conquerors.

Pomegranate Publishing agree with this and in the book *Black Gods and Civilization in Ancient India* by Gert Muller, point out that fire altars, critical to the practice of Hinduism, do not appear in the Indus Valley cities. Moreover, Indra, a key Hindu deity does not appear also. On the other hand, deities that do not appear in the early Aryan literature of the *Rig Veda* can be found in the Indus Valley cities, such as Shiva.

This raises a key question: What religion did the early inhabitants of the India and Pakistan regions originally practice?

Swami Muktananda (1908-1982) has done much to research, write and popularise the pre-Hindu teachings of the region. According to him, Shaivism, i.e. the worship of Lord Shiva, is the early religion of the region.

The main deities were Shiva (male) and Shakti (female). There are many other deities including Vishnu (male) and Sattva (female). These deities later reappear with new additions in Hinduism. This is why there is so much misleading information about the relationship of the Indus Valley civilisation to Hinduism.

Some of the religious ideas of Shaivism can be represented by a female serpent called Kundalini. We can think of Kundalini as a snake crawling up an individual's spine which connects the base of the spine to the pineal gland. The point of the religion was to "awaken kundalini," also called "breaking the chakras". These phrases signify the processes involved in becoming enlightened. There were six main chakras. According to Muktananda, there was the muladhara chakra (at the base of the spine), the svadisthana chakra (between the naval and the genitals), the manipura chakra (near the naval), the anahata chakra (near the heart), the vishudda chakra (near the throat,) and the ajna (or guru) chakra (which is the pineal gland), the seat of Shiva.

Muktananda taught that there were a number of traditional ways to awaken kundalini or break the chakras. He lists these as pryanama (breath control), correct diet, cleansing practices, meditation, and correct living. Finally, he states that Yoga is an important part of the story. There is Bhakti Yoga (devotion to God), Hatha Yoga (different exercises), Laya Yoga (meditation) and Tantric Yoga (sexual energy).

CHAPTER SIX: WHAT IS HINDUISM?

Hinduism came together around 1500 BC. Formulated by the Aryan conquerors of the Indus Valley civilisation, they borrowed ideas from Shaivism and reworked them. They also created a body of literature called the *Rig Veda.* Originally an oral literature, it has since been written down in the language of the Aryans--Sanskrit. It is well known that Sanskrit is related to European languages.

The new religion has three main deities who could be called a Holy Trinity. Brahma is the creator, Vishnu is the preserver, and Shiva is the destroyer.

Another feature of the new religion was the Hindu Caste System. This was a colour and shade based system of racism sharing many features that would pre-empt the *apartheid* system that flourished in South Africa until 1994. There were four main castes. At the top of the pyramid was the Brahmin caste, beneath these were the Khyshatriya caste, then came the Vaisha caste, and at the bottom was the Sudra caste. The indigenous pre-Aryan people became the Sudras. Eventually, another group was added to the system known as the Outcastes or Untouchables. Some of these individuals were people of Aryan and Dravidian admixture. Consequently, some Outcasts were lighter in complexion than the Sudras. Also, over the last three and a half thousand years of Hindu history there has been a great deal of blurring that has taken place between the Aryan and Dravidian populations. This means that one can easily find examples of dark-skinned Brahmins and also light-skinned Sudras. However, in modern India there is still clearly a general relationship between light skin and power, also dark skin and poverty.

According to V. T. Rajshekar, the Aryans came up with a clever way to entice the Dravidians to practice Hinduism even though it was oppressive to them. "They promoted and popularise a Black tribal hero (Krishna) and elevated him to godhood to woo back the Sudras and other masses."

There is an ancient Hindu epic called *Mahabharata*. Several times longer than *The Odyssey* of Homer, one of its many episodes tells of a Black warrior from about 1200 BC who stood up to the invading Aryan forces and

Figure 16. Fresco of Krishna in the City Palace, Udaipur in Rajastan, fourteenth century AD.

killed in battle. No one knows who this warrior was so he was simply referred to as the Black one. In Sanskrit one of the words denoting blackness is 'Krishna'. Eventually, Krishna became an earthly manifestation of Vishnu in Hinduism.

What do we know about Krishna? In the early nineteenth century, when information and documents came to be studied by European scholars about the non-Abrahamic religions, some interesting research was conducted into Hinduism. The erudite English magistrate, Godfrey Higgins, summarise some of these findings which I quote below:

> These observations being premised respecting the Bhagavat Geeta, we will now consider some of the leading facts which are stated in it relating to the God Cristna, Crisna, or Chrishna. These we shall find are copies of the Christian gospel histories, or the Christian gospel histories are copies from them, or they have both been copied from an older mythos. In the first place, the Cristna of India is always represented as a Saviour or Preserver of man-kind, precisely the same as Jesus Christ. While he is thus described as a Saviour, he is also represented to be really the Supreme Being, taking upon himself the state of man: that is, to have become *incarnate in the flesh,* to save the human race, precisely as Jesus is said to have done, by the professors of the orthodox Christian faith. This is the *Verbum caro factum est* of St. John, to which I alluded in Book III. Chap. III. Sect. 4. As soon as Cristna was born, be was saluted with a chorus of Deutas or Devatas or Angels, with divine hymns, just as it is related of Jesus in the orthodox Gospel of Luke, ch. ii. 13, 14. He was cradled among shepherds, to whom were first made known the stupendous feats which stamped his character with marks of the divinity. The circumstances here detailed, though not literally the same as those related of Jesus, are so nearly the same, that it is evident the one account has been taken from the other. The reader will remember the verse of the gospel history, *And there were shepherds tending their flocks by night.* Luke ii. 8. Soon after Cristna's birth, be was carried away by night and concealed in a region remote from his natal place, for fear of a tyrant whose destroyer it was foretold be would become; and who had, for that reason, ordered all the male children born at that period to be slain. This story is the subject of an immense sculpture in the cave at Elephanta, where the tyrant is represented destroying the children. The date of this sculpture is lost in the most remote antiquity. It must, at the very latest period, be fixed at least many hundred years previous to the birth of Jesus Christ, as we shall presently see. But with much greater probability thousands instead of hundreds of years might be assigned to its existence. Cristna was, by the male line, of royal descent, though he was actually born in a state the most abject and humiliating-in a dungeon-as Jesus was descended from King David and was born in a cave, used as a stable. The moment Cristna was born, the whole room was splendidly illuminated, and the countenances of his father and mother emitted rays of glory. According to the *Evangelium Infantiae* "Spelunca repleta erat luminibus, lucernarum et candelarum fulgorum excedentibus, et *solari luce* majoribus." Cristna could speak as soon as he was born, and comforted his

mother, as did the infant Jesus, according to the same gospel history. As Jesus was preceded and assisted by his kinsman, John, so Cristna was preceded by his elder brother, Ram, who was born a little time before him, and assisted him in purifying the world, polluted with demons and monsters. Ram was nourished and brought up by the same foster parents as Cristna. Thus the Gospel of James states, that the prophecy of Zachariah and the supernatural pregnancy of his wife being notorious, Herod suspected that John might be the expected Messiah, and commanded him to be delivered up, in order that he might murder him; but Elizabeth had sent him into the wilderness to his cousin, by which means be escaped. Cristna descended into Hades or Hell, and returned to Vaicontha, his proper paradise. One of his epithets was that of a *good shepherd,* which we know was that of Jesus. After his death, like Jesus Christ, he ascended into heaven. From the glory described above, in the Evangelium Infantiae, we see the reason why, in all pictures of the Nativity, the light is made to arise from the body of the infant, and why the father and mother are often depicted with glories round their heads. After the birth of Cristna, the Indian prophet Nared ... having heard of his fame, visited his father and mother at Gokul, examined the stars, &c., and declared him to be of celestial descent. As Mr. Maurice observes, here is a close imitation of the Magi guided by his star and visiting the Infant in Bethlehem. Cristna was said to have been born at Mathura, (pronounced Mattra,) on the river Jumna, where many of his miracles were performed, *and in which at this day he is held in higher veneration than in any other place in Hindostan.* Mr. Maurice says, "The Arabic edition of the Evangelium Infantiae records Matarea, near Hermopolis, in Egypt, to have been the place where the Infant Saviour resided during his absence from the land of Judaea, and until Herod died."

Godfrey Higgins gave yet another example of similarity:

After Cristna came to man's estate, one of his first miracles was the cure of a leper. Matthew (in ch. viii. ver. 3) states an early miracle performed by Jesus to have been exactly similar, viz. the cure of a leper. Upon another occasion a woman poured on the head of Cristna a box of ointment, for which he cured her of her ailment. Thus, in like manner, a woman came and anointed the head of Jesus. Matt. xxi.7.

Higgins presents another similarity and ends with a powerful question:

Finally, Cristna was put to death by being *crucified;* he descended into hell, and afterward ascended into heaven. For further particulars, see Maurice's Ind. Ant. Vol. 11. pp. 149, &c. The descent into hades or hell, and the ascent into paradise or heaven, is stated by Mr. Maurice; the crucifixion is not stated by him; but my authority for the assertion I shall adduce presently. It is impossible for any one to deny the close connexion between the histories of Jesus and of Cristna. We now come to the most important point--how such connexion is to be rendered consistent with the existence of the whole of the Christian system as at present expounded by our priests,--how the priests are to explain it away.

One modern theologian, Professor Robert Beckford chose to engage with the information. In his powerful television documentary, he summarises his thoughts on the similarities between Krishna and Jesus:

> When I was a child at Sunday School, I was taught very little about other religions. Instead, I was told repeatedly that the Christian story of Jesus was totally unique and that there was only one way to salvation through Him. Anything else was entertaining evil ... To celebrate Krishna's birthday, just like we do at Christmas, Hindus also build Nativity cribs ... The more I looked at it, the more similarities I found between Krishna and Jesus and the more I realised that Jesus' story may not be unique.

CHAPTER SEVEN: WHAT WAS BUDDHISM?

According to the Indian scholar V. T. Rajshekar:

> The Buddha, a great tribal chieftain with an Afro hairstyle, 2,500 years ago was the first to lead India's Black untouchable's war against Aryan oppressors. Buddhism, India's first really virulent anti-Brahmin philosophy, achieved big successes, and the lower caste people and women became its first adherents.

The family of Gautama Siddharta, the person who would become the Buddha, were royalty. Thus the young Gautama had a rich and comfortable upbringing. How do we explain this? In my opinion, even under the old *apartheid*-ruled South Africa, some Black people did rise to positions of power and influence. I believe this was also the case with Gautama's family. However, as V. T. Rajshekar pointed out, he denounced Hinduism and the Caste System.

Pomegranate Publishing present two other opinions that are worth considering. Some Indian scholarship says that Buddha was of indigenous origins but from a ruling family. The only reason Hindus claim him to be a high caste Hindu with the caste position of Kshatriya, is purely based on being from a ruling family, even though he was in fact a non-Aryan.

Other Indian scholarship claims that Buddha was an Aryan. However, even this scholarship agrees that the Aryan clan to which Buddha allegedly belonged, the Shakyas, had intermarried with non-Aryan peoples. In consequence of this, the Shakyas are banned from intermarrying with other Aryan clans.

What do we know about the Buddha? According to Professor John G. Jackson in his masterly text *Christianity Before Christ,* there are some interesting facts about the Buddha. His mother was called Maya. He was the product of a miraculous birth. He was of royal stock. He could speak as soon as he was born and comforted his mother. He was tempted by the Evil One.

Professor Robert Beckford adds that:

> We've already heard of the remarkable similarities between the life stories of Krishna and of Jesus, but here in India there's another important religious

Figure 17. Reclining Buddha in Anuradhapura, Sri Lanka.

> figure. Also the result of a miraculous birth, who was tempted by the Devil before beginning his public ministry at the age of thirty, who performed miracles such as walking on water and the feeding the five hundred, and who challenged the established religious order and presented an alternative way of understanding the world, and who spread his teachings and wisdom through parables and sayings.

Incidentally a number of web pages have attempted to rubbish the alleged similarities between the Jesus and Buddha stories. On one of the pages, *Buddha vs Jesus* on the Tekton Apologetics site, a valiant Christian makes the following claim:

> [H]istory-of-religions scholar David Adams Leeming ... begins his article by pointing out that all 'virgin births' are NOT necessarily such: "A virgin is someone who has not experienced sexual intercourse, and a virgin birth, or parthenogenesis (Gr., parthenos, "virgin"; genesis, "birth"), is one in which a virgin gives birth. According to this definition, the story of the birth of Jesus is a virgin birth story whereas the birth of the Buddha and of Orphic Dionysos are not. Technically what is at issue is the loss or the preservation of virginity during the process of conception. The Virgin Mary was simply "found with child of the Holy Ghost" before she was married and before she had "known" a man. So, too, did the preexistent Buddha enter the womb of his mother, but since she was already a married woman, there is no reason to suppose she was a virgin at the time.

On the same web page, is the following data:

> A reader has noted that Jerome in *Against Jovinianus* Book 1 stated that among the Gymnosophists of India, there was a tradition of Buddha being born from a virgin. But the data clearly shows Jerome to have been either misinformed or else reporting a later tradition, perhaps influenced by Christian missions which had by then penetrated considerably into India.

I am of the opinion, that when one is a hole, it is a good idea to stop digging. St Jerome is the author of the Latin Vulgate version of the Bible. If he states that there is an Indian tradition that Buddha was born from a virgin, then that ends the discussion. The only point that I would like to add is the same one that I made concerning Gerald Massey's similarities between the Christian and the Ancient Egyptian stories. The differences between the Buddha story and the Christian one far outweigh the similarities. However, as I said before, it is not scholarly to ignore the similarities altogether.

Godfrey Higgins, who I have cited several times in this paper, drew some very interesting conclusions that have never been given the intellectual attention it deserves. In his own words:

> Buddha was adored as a square black stone; so was Mercury; so was the Roman Terminus. The famous Pessinuntian stone, brought to Rome, was square and black. The sacred black stone at Mecca many of my readers are acquainted with, and George the Fourth did very wisely to be crowned on the square stone, nearer black than any other colour, of Scotia and Ireland ... Pausanias states the Thespians to have had a temple and statue to Jupiter the Saviour, and a statue to Love, consisting only of a rude stone; and a temple to Venus Melainis, or *the black.* Ammon was founded by Black doves ... One of them flew from Ammon to Dodona and founded it. At Corinth there was a black Venus. In my search into the origin of ancient Druids, I continually found, at last, that my labours termininated with something *black*. Thus the oracles at Dodona, and of Apollo at Delphi, were founded by BLACK doves. Doves are not often, I believe never really, black. Osiris and his Bull were black; all the Gods and Goddesses of Greece were black: at least this was the case with Jupiter, Bacchus, Hercules, Apollo, Ammon. The Goddesses Venus, Isis, Hecati, Diana, Juno, Metis, Ceres, Cybile, are black. The Multimammia is black in the Campidoglio at Rome ... The Linghams in India, anointed with oil, are black: a black stone was adored in numbers of places in India ... On the colour of the Gods of the ancients, and of the identity of them all with the God Sol, and with the Cristna of India, nothing more need be said. The reader has already seen the striking marks of similarity in the history of Cristna and the stories related of Jesus in the Romish [i.e. Roman Catholic] and heretical books. He probably will not think that their effect is destroyed, as Mr. Maurice flatters himself, by the word Cristna in the Indian language signifying black, and the God being of that colour, when he is

Figure 18. The Buddha (twelfth century).

> informed, of what Mr. Maurice was probably ignorant, that in all the Romish countries of Europe, in France, Italy, Germany, &c., the God Christ, as well as his mother, are described in their old pictures and statues to be black.

What Godfrey Higgins is referring to here, is the fact that earlier scholars such as Count De Volney incorrectly believed that there was a linguistic connection between 'Christ' and 'Krishna'. Earlier scholars therefore believed that the two deities both have the same names and were connected with each other. When it was revealed that Krishna actually meant 'black,' many Christian scholars breathed a collective sigh of relief because of course, Christ does not mean black. It actually means 'anointed.' Many Christian scholars therefore hoped that Christ clearly wasn't Black either. Godfrey Higgins, however, proves that there is far more to it than that. In his own words:

> The infant God in the arms of his black mother, his eyes and drapery white, is himself perfectly black. If the reader doubt my word, he may go to the cathedral at Moulins--to the famous chapel of the Virgin at Loretto--to the church of the Annunciata--the church of St. Lazaro, or the church of St. Stephen at Genoa--to St. Francisco at Pisa--to the church at Brixen, in the Tyrol, and to that at Padua--to the church of St. Theodore, at Munich, in the two last of which the whiteness of the eyes and teeth, and the studied redness of the lips, are very observable;--to a church and to the cathedral at Augsburg, where are a black virgin and child as large as life:--to Rome, to the Borghese chapel Maria Maggiore--to the Pantheon--to a small chapel of St. Peter's, on the right-hand side on entering, near the door; and, in fact, to almost innumerable other churches, in countries professing the Romish religion. There is scarcely an old church in Italy where some remains of the worship of the BLACK VIRGIN and BLACK CHILD are not to be met with. Very often the black figures have given way to white ones, and in these cases the black ones, as being held sacred, were put into retired places in the churches, but were not destroyed, but are yet to be found there. In many cases the images are painted all over and look like bronze, often with coloured aprons or napkins round the loins or other, parts; but pictures in great numbers are to be seen, where the white of the eyes and of the teeth, and the lips a little tinged with red, like the black figures in the Museum of the India Company, shew that there is no imitation of bronze. In many instances these images and pictures are shaded, not all one colour, of very dark brown, so dark as to look like black. They are generally esteemed by the rabble with the most profound veneration. The toes are often white, the brown or black paint being kissed away by the devotees, and the white wood left. No doubt in many places, when the priests have new-painted the images, they have coloured the eyes, teeth, &c., in order that they might not shock the feelings of devotees by a too sudden change from black to white, and in order, at the same time, that they might furnish a decent pretence for their blackness, viz. that they are an imitation of bronze: but the number that are left with white teeth, &c., let out the secret.

Understandably, few scholars have attempted to follow up on these ideas of Godfrey Higgins. The reader is referred to yet another book by Pomegranate Publishing for further data on this particular topic entitled *The Black Madonna, Christ, and the Black God and Goddess of the Bible* by Gert Muller.

BIBLIOGRAPHY

Abu ‘Uthman ‘Amr Ibn Bahr Al-Jahiz, *The Book of the Glory of the Blacks,* (Translated by Vincent J. Cornell), US, William Preston, 1990, p.50

Al-Jahiz (776-869), *Al-Fakhar al-Sudan min al-Abyadh (the prides of blacks over the whites),* see https://sites.google.com/site/historyofeastafrica/al-jahiz-al-fakhar-al-sudan

Robert Beckford, *The Hidden Story of Jesus* (documentary), UK, Juniper Communications, 2007

Yosef ben-Jochannan, *African Origins of the Major ‘Western’ Religions,* US, Black Classic Press, 1970, pp.195-218

S. G. Blaxland-Stubbs, *Wonder Cities of Most Ancient India,* in *Wonders of the Past: Second Volume,* ed Sir J. A. Hammerton, UK, The Amalgamated Press, no date given but probably 1937, p.659

C. E. Bosworth et al, *Encyclopedia of Islam, Volume V*, Netherlands, E. J. Brill, 1983, p.705

J. C. deGraft-Johnson, *African Glory,* UK, Watts & Co., 1954, pp.61-64, 65-74, 97

Count de Volney, *The Ruins of Empires,* US, Peter Ecker, 1890, pp.159-160

Cheikh Anta Diop, *The African Origin of Civilization: Myth or Reality?* US, Lawrence Hill Books, 1974, p.128

Peter Garlake, *Early Art and Architecture of Africa,* UK, Oxford University Press, 2002, p.75

Edward Gibbon, *The Decline and Fall of the Roman Empire,* Chapter 50, see http://www.ccel.org/g/gibbon/decline/volume2/chap50.htm

Hazrat Sayedna Bilal Habashi, see http://www.alahazrat.net/islam/hazrat-sayedna-bilal-habashi.php

Godfrey Higgins, *Anacalypsis, Volume I,* UK, Longman, Rees, Orme, Brown & Green, 1836, pp.58, 129-130, 131, 137-138

History for the Relaxed Historian, *Muhammad's Farewell Sermon,* see http://www.emersonkent.com/speeches/farewell_sermon_muhammad.htm

Islamic Architecture History, see http://www.islamic-architecture.info/A-HIST.htm

Islamic Encyclopedia, *Muhammad (570-630 CE)* [sic], see http://islamicencyclopedia.org/public/index/topicDetail/id/694

Islamic Guidance, *Bilal Ibn Rabah RA,* see http://www.islamicguidance.co/#!thecompanions/cuy0

Islamo-Criticism, *Muhammad's Farewell Sermon: "A White has No Superiority Over a Black", A Proven Fabrication,* 11 April 2012, see http://islamo-criticism.blogspot.co.uk/2012/04/muhammads-farewell-sermon-white-has-no.html

John G. Jackson, *Christianity Before Christ,* US, American Atheist Press, 1985, pp.79-90

John G. Jackson, *Man, God, and Civilization,* US, Citadel Press, 1972, p.247

Tahar Labib ed., *Imagining the Arab Other: How Arabs and Non-Arabs Represent Each Other,* UK, I. B. Tauris, 2007, p.114

D. S. Margoliouth, *Mohammed and the Rise of Islam,* UK, G. P. Putnam's Sons, 1905, p.49

Gert Muller, *Black Gods and Civilization of Ancient India,* UK, Pomegranate Publishing, 2013, pp.19-20, 78-83

Gert Muller, *The Black Madonna, Christ, and the Black God and Goddess of the Bible,* UK, Pomegranate Publishing, 2013, pp.3-57

Swami Muktananda, *Play of Consciousness,* US, Siddha Yoga Publications, 1978

Adib Rashad, *African Contributions to the Rise of Islam,* 2005, see http://www.africanholocaust.net/news_ah/africa_contribution_islam.htm

V. T. Rajshekar, *The Black Untouchables of India: Reclaiming our cultural heritage,* in *African Presence in Early Asia,* ed Runoko Rashidi, US, Transaction Publishers, 1995, pp.235, 238

Runoko Rashidi, *African Star Over Asia,* UK, Books of Africa, 2015, pp.116, 117, 170

J. A. Rogers, *World's Great Men of Color, Volume 1,* US, Macmillan, 1972, p.168

Tekton Apologetics, *Buddha vs Jesus,* see http://tektonics.org/copycat/buddha02.php

Dawud Walid, *7 Luminous Black Companions of the Prophet,* 20 February 2015, see http://muslimmatters.org/2015/02/20/7-luminous-black-companions-of-the-prophet/

Robin Walker, *When We Ruled: Second Edition,* UK, Reklaw Education, 2013, pp.424-525, 542-558

Wikipedia, *Adhan,* see https://en.wikipedia.org/wiki/Adhan

Wikipedia, *Bilal Ibn Rabah,* see https://en.wikipedia.org/wiki/Bilal_Ibn_Rabah

Wikipedia, *Dhul-Nun al-Misri,* see https://en.wikipedia.org/wiki/Dhul-Nun_al-Misri

PART FOUR

BLACK INFLUENCES IN THE ORIGIN OF THE NEW RELIGIOUS MOVEMENTS

INTRODUCTION

In the earlier parts of this book, I showed that Black people were amongst the movers and shakers in the origin and evolution of the religions that became Judaism, Christianity and Islam. In my earlier book *Blacks and Religion Volume One,* I make a bigger claim. I show that the very earliest religious ideas of the human species were created wholly by Black people.

In Part One of this book, I demonstrated that Black people influenced the origin and evolution of Judaism. For instance, Amen, the ancient Nile Valley deity, is to be found in Judaism. Circumcision, an ancient African practice, is practised in Judaism. The 42 Declarations of Innocence profoundly influenced the teaching of ethical behaviour in Judaism. Ancient Egyptian texts and stories influenced the Flood Story, the Birth of Moses story, Proverbs 22 and Psalms 104. Moreover, some of the early personalities in the origin and evolution of Judaism were Black. Moses, if he existed, was an Ancient Egyptian. The people of the Kingdom of Judah in 700 BCE were Negroes. Finally, the people of the Elephantine Island synagogue must have been Ancient Egyptians and/or Kushites.

In Part Two of the book, I demonstrated that Black people influenced the origin and evolution of Christianity. Amen, Osiris, Isis, and Horus, are all to be found in Christianity albeit in a somewhat disguised form. Ancient Egyptian beliefs and practices profoundly influenced Christian festivals and practices such as Lent, the Eucharist and Baptism. The icons, Mary and Jesus, were originally derived from the Nile Valley icons of Isis and Horus. Some of the early personalities in the origin and evolution of Christianity were Africans including Tertullian, Namphamo, St Perpetua, Felicitas, St Cyprian, St Augustine, Emperor Ezana, St Anthony and St Pachomius.

In Part Three of the book, I demonstrated that Black people influenced the origin and evolution of Islam, especially Ethiopians and Black Arabs. The Ethiopians offered sanctuary to some of the earliest followers of the Prophet. Ethiopian architects built Mecca in an indigenous style. Some of the beliefs and practices in Islam come from African culture filtered through Judaism and Christianity such as the wearing of the veil. There were great Negroes in the history of Islam including the Prophet's father, some of the Companions of the Prophet, Bilal, Dhu l'Nun and Mansa Musa I.

However, it must be stressed throughout that these religions are not completely African. It is best to present these as syntheses of some African ideas and some non-African ideas. Amongst the most important non-African ideas in these religions are the Chosen People myth, the anti-female sexism, and the belief in the separation between God and humans.

This has led many Black people in more recent times to raise big and difficult questions of which way forward should we go with religion? Other key questions that have been raised are: Should we self-consciously Africanise Judaism, Christianity or Islam? Should we reject them and reclaim African Traditionalism? Should we create something new? Should we reject religion entirely? Should we continue just as we are?

CHAPTER ONE: THE EARLY ANTECEDENTS

In the history of Islam, two African men seized the initiative and proclaimed themselves to be the Mahdi, or the expected Messiah.

Lady Lugard in her masterpiece, *A Tropical Dependency,* tells of the great Moroccan Mahdi of the twelfth century, Ibn Tumart.

> In the same spirit of religious reform which had stirred the founder of the Almoravide sect, a Mahdi arose in the earlier part of the twelfth century in the northern provinces of Ifrikiah, and preached a doctrine so stringent that he excited a revolt among the populace, and was obliged to fly from the anger of the Sultan. He appeared first in Bugia in 1118, and preached his ascetic reforms in Telemçan, Fez, Mequinez, and Morocco. Everywhere he excited the anger of the people, and towards 1121 he withdrew into the desert, where gradually disciples began to join him in great numbers. The authorities persecuted him here also, and he then called upon the Mesmudian Berbers to rally to his cause, to defend his person, and to declare a Holy War in defence of the doctrine of the Unity of God. He declared himself to be the Mahdi, and he gave to his followers the title of Almohades or Unitarians. He entrenched himself in the Mountain of Tinmelel in the southern fastnesses of the Atlas chain, and this spot remained the stronghold of the sect until their final extinction as a political power about a hundred years later. The original Mahdi died in 1128, but this event had little effect upon the sect.

Professor Cheikh Anta Diop in his book, *Precolonial Black Africa,* tells of the great Sudanese Mahdi of the nineteenth century.

> The Mahdi, according to Muslim tradition, is the Messiah, the Saviour who, before the end of the world, will bring the entire earth to Islam. Proclaiming himself such, one Mohammed Ahmed, a Sudanese by origin, galvanized his men, and succeeded in defeating Rashid-Bey, the governor of Fashoda. In 1882, he defeated an Egyptian column and occupied all the Kordofan: he completely massacred an army of ten thousand men commanded by Hicks Pasha. In 1883, Slatin Pasha, the British governor of Darfur, and Lupton-Bey (the British governor of Bahr-el-Ghazal, who affected Arab aliases as did the former) were also beaten by him. They capitulated in 1884. He conquered the Berber country as well as the Sennar. On January 26, 1885, he entered the citadel of Khartoum and there slew Gordon Pasha (Chinese Gordon). Eight-tenths of the Sudanese territory had been reconquered from the Anglo-Egyptian coalition opposing the Sudanese Blacks, when he died. His victory was the

> more valiant in that the victorious Sudanese had only bows and arrows while the Anglo-Egyptians were equipped with the most modern firearms available.

Professor Jan Vansina in his book, *Kingdoms of the Savannah,* tells of a Kongolese aristocrat and Christian prophetess called Donna Beatriz (or Kimpa Vita):

> Around 1700 a woman prophet began to claim that she was in contact with heaven and especially with St. Anthony [i.e. NOT the St Anthony of Upper Egypt] and that it was her mission to find a man who would bring an end to the wars and restore the kingship. In this she was not unlike Joan of Arc. But her teaching was also pervaded with elements which are now attributed to modern movements such as the so-called African "Zionist churches." She said that Christ was black and that heaven was for the Africans, that people should not listen to the foreign missionary but to her and to her catechists. The movement was finally stopped when the prophetess was condemned and burned for heresy.

In nineteenth century America, an African American theologian, Bishop Henry McNeal Turner was instrumental in popularising an idea known as the 'Ethiopianist' doctrine. Inspired by the Biblical passage "Princes shall come of Egypt; Ethiopia shall soon stretch out her hands unto God" (Psalms, 68:31), many saw this as a prophecy that Africa would "soon" experience dramatic political, industrial and economic renaissance. "Ethiopianism" was particularly popular in South Africa where hundreds of churches were formed around that idea. Many of these churches were heavily influenced by Henry McNeal Turner who visited South Africa and urged that religious independence must precede and lay the foundation for political independence.

The Bishop had other radical ideas reported by Wikipedia. At a February 1898 convention, he said:

> We have as much right biblically and otherwise to believe that God is a Negro, as you buckra or white people have to believe that God is a ... white man. For the bulk of you and all the fool Negroes of the country believe that God is white-skinned, blue eyed, straight-haired, projected nosed, compressed lipped ... white gentleman, sitting upon a throne somewhere in the heavens. Every race of people who have attempted to describe their God by words, or by paintings, or by carvings, or any other form or figure, have conveyed the idea that the God who made them and shaped their destinies was symbolized in themselves, and why should not the Negro believe that he resembles God?

Some of these ideas were taken up and developed by the Honourable Marcus Garvey between 1914 and 1928. According to Professor Maulana

Figure 19. The Honourable Marcus Garvey flanked by senior U. N. I. A. members.

Karenga, Garvey played a key role in the establishment of liberation theologies for Black people. That role was explicitly remembered and acknowledged by the adherents of Rastafari and the Moorish Science Temple of America.

As the leader of the Universal Negro Improvement Association and African Communities League, the Honourable Marcus Garvey led the biggest movement of Black people in history with an international membership of 6 million people.

As a religious leader, Garvey brought the Ethiopian Coptic Church to the African Diaspora. A colleague of his within the movement, Bishop Alexander McGuire, headed the Diasporan Church. Garvey taught that God has no colour. However, Black people should see God through Ethiopian eyes. Therefore Black people have a right and a responsibility to see God as Black. He also taught that Jesus was a Black revolutionary standing up to the oppressive White power structure in his time, the Roman Empire. This is similar to what Marcus Garvey himself was doing in his time, standing up to global European power.

Garvey combined these religious ideas with a political programme based around the principle of Race First. There was also an economic programme based on the ideas of Booker T. Washington but expanded to build global self-sufficiency among Black people. There was a cultural programme based around the principles of African Fundamentalism. These ideas shared some similarities with Negritude, Afrocentrism and African Centredness of later periods.

In a previous part of this book, we saw that there is much controversy over whether or not the Exodus story really happened as described in the Bible. However, it is no secret that Black people were enslaved in the Americas for 400 years. Consequently, many people have suggested that the story of the Children of Israel being enslaved in Egypt for 400 years did not literally happen but were in fact prophecies of what would happen to Black people in Africa, who would become the Diaspora. This implies, according to some theological thinkers, that Black people are indeed the Chosen People represented in the Bible. Three particular movements were inspired in part by this idea, Rastafari, the Moorish Science Temple of America, and The Lost Found Nation of Islam in the West.

CHAPTER TWO: RASTAFARI

Professor Leonard Barrett and the Dub poet Yasus Afari in their respective books tell us that The Honourable Marcus Garvey was an important figure in the evolution of Rastafari. In 1916, he is said to have made a controversial but impactful prophecy. Some quote him as saying: "Look to the East where a Black king will be crowned. He shall be the Redeemer." On 2 November 1930, there was a spectacular coronation of the new Emperor of Ethiopia. Called "Haile Selassie", the Emperor's name in his local Amharic language meant 'Power' or 'Might of the Trinity'. He was also called "Ras Tafari". Ras meant 'Duke' or 'Head'. Tafari meant 'Creator'. These names were interpreted by many as proof that Haile Selassie was indeed a Divine personage.

Revelations 19:16 in the Bible states that when the Messiah returns on his vesture and on his thigh will be a name: King of Kings, and Lord of Lords. Something like this actually occurred during the coronation of the Ethiopian Emperor. Revelations 5:5 mentions the Lion of the Tribe of Judah will be able to open the scroll and its seven seals. It turns out, that Lion of Judah is one of the Ethiopian Emperor's titles. Daniel 7:9 contains a prophecy about a coming King who will have hair like lamb's wool and whose throne was like a fiery flame. Again, Haile Selassie could be said to have matched this description.

In Jamaica, four priests with theological backgrounds grounded in the Bible came together to become founders of Rastafari in late 1930. Inspired by Marcus Garvey's prophecy, these four men, Leonard Howell, Joseph Hibbert, Archibald Dunkley, and Robert Hinds were looking to the East for a Black king to be crowned. Haile Selassie's coronation seemed to fulfil various Biblical prophecies. Thus was born the Rastafari religion.

According to a British Government census, over three quarters of Jamaica in 1944 was of unmixed African descent. That reality was NOT reflected in the Jamaican power structure which was largely dominated by individuals that were more mixed with European, Lebanese, and other exotic ancestry. This resulted in considerable social prejudice against dark skinned individuals and resulted in a colour and shade hierarchy that has only been challenged within the last 20 years. Thus Jamaica lacked genuine Black power until relatively recently. Thus Rastafari became a voice for the poor and dispossessed Black people of Jamaica who denounced the oppressive ruling classes as 'Babylon'. In response, the lighter skinned Jamaican ruling classes discriminated against Rastafari seeing it as a dangerous, dope smoking, counter cultural cult. Since Rastafari preached a pro African and pro Black message, this shocked many light-skinned Jamaicans who did not want to be associated with anything that was associated with Africa. As Rastafari spread across the Caribbean, some of the other Caribbean islands took equally repressive measures against this dangerous pro African religion.

Why did the practitioners of Rastafari wear their hair as dreadlocks? Practitioners of Rastafari told me the following. During the Mau Mau Rebellion in Kenya against the extraordinarily cruel British oppression, many Jamaicans were impressed by the defiant appearance of one of Jomo Kenyatta's generals. The General had long and prominent locks. Since the Bible teaches that one should not mar one's hair or beard, this provided the rationale for Rastas to not cut or comb their hair. Thus the Mau Mau general became a role model for Rasta appearance. The textbooks on Rastafari, however, tell a different story. According to Yasus Afari:

> During the Italian occupation of Ethiopia (1936-41), the loyal RASES, soldiers, guerrilla fighters, patriots and other able-bodied Ethiopians under the Supreme Command of H.I.M., waged a relentless warfare to repel the fascist Italian forces. The news and war reports coming out of Ethiopia carried pictures of Ethiopian warriors, priests and other citizens, with dread locks.

What do the Rastas believe? Influenced by the Biblical passage, "Princes shall come of Egypt; Ethiopia shall soon stretch out her hands unto God", Rastas see the Bible as originally teaching a Black religion. They argue that, in a world dominated by white supremacy; this fact has been buried and obscured. They also believe that Babylon represents the oppressive structures under which Black people live. When they coined this term, they did not just mean Europe and Europeans. They also included the light-skinned Jamaican power structure. In the early days of Rasta, the followers believed that they will be repatriated to Africa. Some were more specific and located the Holy Land as Ethiopia. Rastas adopted the red, green and gold colours of the Ethiopian flag.

Rastas believe that words have power to elevate or oppress people. Consequently, they believe that many English words have dual meanings that can result in the people bringing themselves and each other down through lack of understanding. For example, the word 'understanding' contains the words 'under' and 'stand'. Rastas prefer to say 'overstanding' instead. The first syllable of the word 'oppression,' according to Rastas, is the word 'up'. Rastas prefer to say 'down'. Consequently they say 'down-pression'.

In April 1966 His Imperial Majesty Haile Selassie visited Jamaica. His visit electrified the crowds who lined the streets to see him chanting "Jah Rastafari!" Many regard this as a defining moment in the evolution of Rastafari. Haile Selassie is said to have given the following message to his followers of the need to liberate Jamaica first and then come to Africa. Thus Rasfari must oppose oppressive structures under which Black people live where ever we are. This is a prerequisite for returning to Africa.

However as early as 1937, Haile Selassie did set aside 500 acres land in Ethiopia's Goba Valley for Black Diasporans who wanted to return to Africa. This territory, Shasemani, is inhabited and worked by Black Diasporans to this very day.

Rastafari was an important contributor to the origin and evolution of the Jamaican musical form, Reggae. Most of the leading reggae artists were practitioners of the religion. Among these were Toots and the Maytals, Jimmy Cliff, The Wailers, Jacob Miller, Mystic Revelation of Rastafari, et cetera. The leading reggae artists of today still have the link with Rastafari such as Capleton. Garveyism, Black consciousness, and Rastafari redemption were key themes in reggae lyrical material. This musical form put Jamaica on the cultural world map. It also put Rastafarianism on the religious world map.

Dr Vernon Carrington, also known as Prophet Gad, created a new house within Rasta called the Twelve Tribes in the 1970s. Within this movement, followers received a new name based on the Twelve Tribes of Israel in the Bible. Due to the influence of the reggae musicians Bob Marley and Dennis Brown, this house spread quickly across the world. According to Afari, its moderate, middle-of-the-road stance was popular with middle-class people. There were even many White converts to the Twelve Tribes movement all over the world. The Twelve Tribes inclusive multiracial Rastafari is one of the most successful and fastest-growing livities in history. Like Buddhism before it, it was spread by the positivity of its message and the livity that it produced, and not by the sword.

According to Professor Barrett, the Twelve Tribes have a number of practices that distinguishes them from earlier forms of Rastafari. They

Figure 20. Joseph Hibbert, one of the founders of Rastafari.

encourage daily Bible study, consider mystical ideas surrounding the number 12 and the Zodiac, believe that only 144,000 people will be chosen in the afterlife, see Haile Selassie and Jesus Christ as interchangeable concepts, see Dr Carrington as the Prophet, collect regular membership dues, hold monthly dances based on roots reggae, and give men and women equal roles within the movement.

The older Black power Rastafarians became known as the Order of Niah Binghi. Most of these argue that White people have no place in Rastafari. With the slogan “death to all down pressers”, whether White or Black, they continue to fight for Black liberation, reparations, repatriation and what they call Rastafarian Inity (i.e. unity).

CHAPTER THREE: THE MOORISH SCIENCE TEMPLE OF AMERICA

The Moorish Science Temple of America was started by Timothy Drew in 1913 in Newark, New Jersey. Professor C. Eric Lincoln reports a legend that Drew visited Egypt and later Mecca some time before this period. In Mecca, Drew was given the name Sharif Abdul Ali. When anglicised, this name became Noble Drew Ali, the name by which Drew would be better known. In a dream, Drew was chosen to restore the Lost Found Nation to their natural religion. Drew would call the formerly enslaved and kidnapped people the Asiatics or Moors. He saw his mission as restoring the religious heritage and culture of this lost nation.

The Moorish Science Temple of America taught that just as John the Baptist prepared the way for Jesus, Marcus Garvey would prepare the way for Prophet Noble Drew Ali. Thus the ideology of the movement was a synthesis of Islam and Garveyism. Other ideas were clearly influenced by Christianity and other Oriental philosophies.

According to Prophet Noble Drew Ali:

> Islam is a very simple faith. It requires man to recognize his duties toward God Allah, his Creator and his fellow creatures. It teaches the supreme duty of living at peace with one's surroundings. It is pre-eminently the religion of peace. The very name Islam means peace. The goal of man's life according to ISLAM, is peace with everything. Peace with Allah and peace with men. The Koran, the Holy Book of Islam, tells us that the final abode of man is the "House of Peace," where no vain word or sinful discourse will be heard.

However, Ali wrote his own Koran. This document is called *The Holy Koran Circle 7.* In this book, Garvey is portrayed as a forerunner.

Ali taught that his duty as the Prophet was to save the nations from the wrath of Allah. He would uplift the fallen of humanity, especially the Moorish Americans by teaching them to be themselves through their old-time religion which he calls Islamism. They should start using their red flag with its five pointed green star where each point represents love, truth, peace, freedom and justice. Ali taught that Jesus was sent by Allah to save the Israelites from the iron hand oppression of the pale skin nations of Europe who were then ruling in Palestine.

Figure 21. Noble Drew Ali, founder of the Moorish Science Temple of America.

Ali also taught that the dark people of America should renounce names such as Negro, Coloured, Black or Ethiopian. These terms inflicted on dark people by European slavery rob the people of, what he saw as, their history, nationality and heritage. They must refer to themselves as Moors. Moreover, Ali taught that the dark people of America, like dark people everywhere are Asiatics. Within this broad category are the Moors, the Egyptians, the Hindus, the Turks, the descendants of Africa, et cetera. How did he come to this conclusion? According to him, the inhabitants of Africa, and for that matter the Prophet Jesus, are descendants of the Ancient Canaanites. Since Canaan is in Western Asia, this is probably the origin of the term Asiatic.

Ali taught that the Moors in America, descendants of Africa, must remain a clean and pure nation with no desire to amalgamate or marry with the families of the pale skin nations of Europe. Neither should they serve the gods of the Europeans. Instead, they should return Christianity back to the pale nations of Europe.

He also taught that there is a higher self and the lower self. The higher self is the moral virtues and the harmonies of life that breed justice, mercy, love and right. Moreover, people can also be representatives of the higher self such as the Asiatics (which includes Moors). The lower self is the devil. It breeds hatred, slander, lewdness, murders, theft, and everything that harms. People can also represent the lower self. Especially those who were cast out of the holy city of Mecca, and those who accept the teachings of those who were cast out.

His movement underwent a massive growth in the late 1920s. The Moorish Science Temple of America spread primarily to the northern cities such as Detroit, Harlem, Chicago, Pittsburgh, and Philadelphia. At its height, the movement may well have had between 20 and 30,000 people.

Professor Maulana Karenga says:

> Ali's basic contentions and principles contributed to the religious philosophy of the Nation of Islam which came into being afterwards. His stress on name, land and nationality, his division of the world into Dark and White peoples, his political conservatism and his conception of divine retribution of Allah on whites, all find subsequent expression in the ideology and practice of the Nation of Islam."

CHAPTER FOUR: THE LOST FOUND NATION OF ISLAM IN THE WEST

The Lost Found Nation of Islam in the West had origins shrouded in controversy. Several writers including Cuba and Karenga trace the origin of this movement to the Moorish Science Temple of America. Noble Drew Ali died in 1929 in contentious circumstances. His movement split into competing factions. Master Fard or Farad Muhammad, a mysterious but influential figure, emerged as head of one of the factions.

The Nation of Islam teach that Farad Muhammad was an Arab born in Mecca on 26 February 1877. He was of mixed ancestry, with a Black father (called Alphonso Shabazz) and a White mother. He came to America with a divine message for Black Americans. His message was that Black Americans are the Chosen People of God and they must return to the religion of their ancestors and reclaim the names of their ancestors. Master Farad Muhammad posed Islam as the religion of the ancestors. He also posed Islamic names as the names of the ancestors. All those who do not know their original names, i.e. the majority of Black Americans, should replace their surnames with the mathematical symbol for the unknown which is an X.

The Nation of Islam say that Farad Muhammad was the founder (or co founder with Elijah Muhammad) of the Lessons, the Fruit of Islam, and the Muslim Girls Training, General Civilisation Classes. Wakeel Allah explained what these were.

The Lessons are a body of material that members of the Nation of Islam are required to learn orally. This teaching method reflects in some ways the methods that would have been used in African secret societies. The student is expected to remember the information without writing any of it down. Wakeel Allah lists a Student Enrolment Lesson, Original Instructions to the Labourers, Lost-Found Muslim Lessons, The Actual Facts, The Problem Book, General Orders, and The Restricted Laws of Islam.

The Fruit of Islam is the security wing of the Nation of Islam. Men are expected to participate in the physical training and self defence classes necessary to build the discipline required for the security wing. They also learn about what it means to be a man and the responsibilities of a husband

Figure 22. The Honourable Elijah Muhammad and Minister Malcolm X.

and father. Other issues that are taught are the importance of honesty, chastity, cleanliness, and correct business principles. The instruction to men stresses why these things are important to a person, a home, a community, a nation, and a civilisation.

Muslim Girls Training and the General Civilization Classes represent the program and training for girls and women. Taught on Thursday nights, this is where the females are instructed in how to keep homes, rear children, care for their husbands, cooking, sewing, et cetera. They are also taught how to act at home and abroad, and other things important to being a good Muslim woman.

On Friday nights, called Civilisation Night, the Nation of Islam taught classes to males and females in the area of domestic relations. The classes stressed why males and females must understand and respect the differences between each other's true natures.

However, Master Farad Muhammad disappeared in 1933 or 34 with as much controversy as he first appeared. No one seems to know what happened to him. Under the leadership of the African American, Elijah Muhammad, the Nation of Islam became an influential force in African American life.

Figure 23. The Fruit of Islam.

Elijah Muhammad had a background as a corporal in the UNIA. He was originally in the Detroit division of one of Garvey's militias. As the leader of the Nation of Islam, he became known as the Messenger of Allah. He wrote a number of books including *The Supreme Wisdom, Message to the Blackman in America, How to Eat to Live,* et cetera.

He taught that the Black people are the original people of the planet Earth. Moreover, Black Americans should stop calling themselves Negroes and start calling themselves Blacks. He taught that Black people are God's Chosen People and that all Black men are potentially Gods. By contrast, White people are actually children of the Devil.

In the Nation of Islam's newspapers, the Messenger listed the demands of the Nation of Islam as *What the Muslims want* and *What the Muslims believe.* The Messenger maintained that Black people should maintain their social separation from Whites to not incur the wrath of Allah and should seek to build institutions of their own. The ultimate aim of the Nation of Islam is for Black Americans to build a nation of their own. That nation could be in Africa, but most of the Nation of Islam's literature is focused on the need to take control of the five Southern states of America.

He taught that heaven and hell exists right here, right now on planet Earth. Heaven is where you have systems and structures that are working for you and your people. Hell is where you do not have these structures and your enemies have them and are using them against you. Thus, the Nation of Islam teach that the White man's heaven is the Black man's hell.

The Nation of Gods and Earths

Pen Black and Wakeel Allah in their respective books tell us that Clarence 13X, later known as Father Allah, was a teacher of karate at Temple Number 7 in Harlem. He left the Nation of Islam in 1963 but some say he was expelled by Minister Malcolm X. He was the first to break away and create an original movement.

A year later and with the help of friends, he started his own movement. Known as the Nation of Gods and Earths or as the 5%ers, this movement attempted to bring the teachings of Elijah Muhammad to the streets. In effect, they had democratised The Lessons. Father Allah aimed to reach the poor, the disenfranchised, and the hard-core street youth. As Pen Black put it: "He saw God's work as teaching the dumb, deaf and blind and from them to raise a Righteous *Nation of Gods and Earths.*"

The name, 5%ers, refers to an idea taught in the Nation of Islam that 85% of Black people are mentally blind. This is also true of the entire planet. This mental blindness means that most people have no real knowledge of their own origin, their true history, nor do they have the correct understanding of God. They are led to believe that they should worship a mystery God that they cannot see. This mental slavery enables them to be used as tools and slaves by those who would deceive them.

The deceivers are the 10%ers. As bloodsuckers of the poor, they thrive as slave makers and benefit from keeping the poor mentally dead. Some of these 10%ers have real knowledge, but they keep it from the masses especially from the Original People. The 10%ers take their cue from the White male power structure, but they can in fact be from any race including Black. One of the main tricks that the 10% teach is that the White image of Christ is the true image. Moreover, they teach that God is a mystery that cannot be mastered but we should worship it anyway.

The 5%ers are the truth bringers. Also called the poor righteous teachers, their role is to uplift the 85% and free them from the false teaching of a White mystery God. The name, Nation of Gods and Earths perhaps needs to be explained. The movement teaches that the original man, the Asiatic Black man, represent the true and living Gods on this planet. This is in line with an idea taught by the Prophet Jesus reported in John 10:34 that "Ye are gods". With this knowledge, the Original People do not need to worship another to find what is inside of themselves. The movement teaches that Black women are Earths. As the Mothers of Civilisation, her rightful place was to be a Queen by the side of Allah. Just as the Earth produces life, so do Black woman.

Afrika Bambaataa is regarded as the Godfather of Hip-Hop Culture. Heavily influenced by the teachings of Clarence 13X, Bambaataa championed the idea that Hip-Hop culture has five elements: (i) DJing, (ii) B-Boying, (iii) Aerosol writing (or Tagging), (iv) MCing (or Rapping), and (v) Knowledge. The Knowledge component was the teachings of Clarence 13X. Consequently, many of the influential figures in Hip-Hop culture were/are members of the Nation of Gods and Earths. Among these are Rakim Allah, Big Daddy Kane, Queen Latifah, Busta Rhymes and Jay Z. Others were influenced by the Nation of Islam including Public Enemy, MC Ren, DMX, Snoop Dogg and Foxy Brown.

Transformation of the original Nation of Islam

On the death of the Messenger of Allah, Elijah Muhammad, his seventh child succeeded him in 1975. This son, Wallace Muhammad, transformed the Nation of Islam. He banned the sale of his father's books, such as *Message to the Blackman in America,* and promoted Orthodox Islam in its place. He discontinued the Fruit of Islam. Moreover, he sold off the business empire that the Nation of Islam had built up. The old Nation of Islam was renamed the World Community of Al-Islam in the West. It has since been renamed the American Muslim Mission.

The old members of the movement by in large agreed to support the new changes. Leaders of congregations, originally called 'Ministers,' were now called 'Imams'. In place of the old pro Black teachings, the movement only used the Qur'an. Unlike orthodox Muslims elsewhere, the movement made no use of the Hadith. It was during this period that the first significant numbers of non-Black people joined the African American movement. The movement continues to flourish today but has largely stayed under the radar.

However in 1977 Imam Silis Muhammad issued a letter to Wallace Muhammad entitled *Declaration of Spiritual War.* He left the movement and brought a number of followers with him. They attempted to rebuild the Nation of Islam along the race first principles laid out by Elijah Muhammad. This was the second significant split since Clarence 13X.

Later in the same year, Louis Farrakhan Muhammad did the same thing. He left the movement and brought an even greater number of followers with him. He attempted to rebuild the Nation of Islam along the principles laid out by Elijah Muhammad achieving some high profile successes. His numbers are bigger that Silas Muhammad's. Moreover, he pulled off the two biggest civil protests in American history: the Million Man March / Day of Absence and the Million Woman March.

CHAPTER FIVE: KINGISM AND BLACK LIBERATION THEOLOGY

The Reverend Dr Martin Luther King was the leader of the Southern Christian Leadership Conference, i.e. the Southern Baptists. His civil protests against injustices led to him being jailed on more than one occasion. In 1963 he composed a letter to explain his philosophies to other churchmen who could not understand what he was doing. This letter, called *Letter from a Birmingham Jail,* lays out the basic principles of Dr King's philosophy of non-violent confrontation.

Dr King believed that Christians must oppose sin. For instance, if someone oppresses you, they are sinning. However, if you let them oppress you, then you are sinning! Consequently, Christians have a duty to oppose oppression otherwise they will be damned as sinners. The most effective way to oppose sin is not through violence, but through non-violent confrontation. Influenced by the practices of Gandhi, King believed that he could shame the American government in the eyes of world public opinion. He would conduct civil protests in the full glare of the world's media. These protests provoked extreme and violent reactions by the forces of the American government, again, in the full glare of the world's media. Dr King further believed that in fighting injustice and oppression, Black Americans would be doing God's work. This would spread a greater Christian civilisation amongst Americans as a whole that would lead to a Christian revival in America.

Dr King's message has been taken up by Reverend Jesse Jackson and Reverend Al Sharpton today. These ideas have also influenced Black Liberation Theology.

Reverend James Cone was the founder of Black Liberation Theology in the 1960s. He taught that God is always on the side of the oppressed and to the extent that Black people are oppressed then, in that eschatological sense, God is Black. He stressed that Black churches should recapture the radical spirit of 19th-century radicals such as Henry Garnett and Nat Turner and champion the struggle for freedom, equality and justice. Cone also denounced the White church, especially in America, as a racist anti-Christ and a tool of oppression that must be opposed. In the United Kingdom

Figure 24. The Reverend Dr Martin Luther King.

much more recently, the brilliant theologian Professor Robert Beckford has advanced and taught some of Reverend Cone's ideas.

Reverend Albert Cleage (also called Jaramogi Ageyman) created the Shrine of the Black Madonna. While he was influenced by the Honourable Elijah Muhammad's teachings, Cleage thought that Islam would only be able to organise only the tiniest fraction of the Black American community. Consequently, Cleage concluded that the Black Church, the only institution owned by Black people, would be the only institution that could liberate Black people from White oppression.

Disagreeing with Reverend Cone, Cleage did not accept that God was Black merely because Black people are oppressed and God is on the side of the oppressed. On the contrary, Cleage held that God was Black because Jesus and the Ancient Israelites were ethnically Black. Consequently, Cleage challenged the monopoly that White Christians and Jews have over the Biblical figures. He went further and argued that the White church presents a dishonest version of the Biblical stories to whiten the Ancient Israelites who were originally Black. Cleage thus argues that Christianity is a Stolen Legacy that the White church has dishonestly appropriated from Black people.

He taught that the Old Testament of the Bible is a story of the struggle of the Black Israelites that provides models for Black Americans today. However, many Christians have been fooled and rendered docile by the Pauline perversions that emphasise loving submission that run through the New Testament. Cleage rejects the teachings of St Paul and believes that

God demands struggle of his Chosen People just like in the Old Testament i.e. an eye for an eye and a tooth for a tooth.

BIBLIOGRAPHY

Yasus Afari, *Overstanding Rastafari,* Jamaica, Senya-Cum, 2007, pp.16, 43, 128-141, 176-189, 192-193, 203-207

Wakeel Allah, *In the Name of Allah,* US, A Team Publishing, 2007, pp.81-85, 137-142

Leonard Barrett, *The Rastafarians,* US, Beacon, 1988, pp.80-247

Pen Black, *Gods Earths and 85ers,* US, Tru Life Publishing, 2007, pp.1-73

Albert B. Cleage Jr., *Black Christian Nationalism,* US, Morrow Quill, 1972, pp.44-76

Prince A. Cuba, *Black Gods of the Inner City,* US, 1992, see https://moorishorthodox.wordpress.com/black-gods/

Timothy Dingle-El-Noble Drew-Ali, *The Resurrection,* US, Prince of Printing Inc., 1995, pp.17, 48-50, 140-147, 232-251, 264-265, 272-273

Cheikh Anta Diop, *Precolonial Black Africa,* US, Lawrence Hill Books, 1987, pp.169-170

Maulana Karenga, *Introduction to Black Studies, Fourth Edition,* US, University of Sankore Press, 2010, pp.141-144, 158-159, 172-175, 218-225, 230-233, 237-239

C. Eric Lincoln, *The Black Muslims in America: Third Edition,* US, Africa World Press, 1994, pp.257, 263-276

Lady Lugard, *A Tropical Dependency, Second Impression,* UK, James Nisbet & Co., 1906, pp.58-59

Martin Luther King Jr., *Letter from a Birmingham Jail,* US, 1963, see https://www.africa.upenn.edu/Articles_Gen/Letter_Birmingham.html

Jan Vansina, *Kingdoms of the Savanna,* US, University of Wisconsin Press, 1966, p.154

Wikipedia, *Henry McNeal Turner,* see https://en.wikipedia.org/wiki/Henry_McNeal_Turner

Also available

PART FIVE

THE AUTHOR

ROBIN WALKER

Biography

Robin Walker 'The Black History Man' was born in London but has also lived in Jamaica. He attended the London School of Economics and Political Science where he read Economics.

In 1991 and 1992, he studied African World Studies with the brilliant Dr Femi Biko and later with Mr Kenny Bakie. Between 1993 and 1994, he trained as a secondary school teacher at Edge Hill College (linked to the University of Lancaster).

Since 1992 and up to the present period, Robin Walker has lectured in adult education, taught university short courses, and chaired conferences in African World Studies, Egyptology and Black History. The venues have been in Toxteth (Liverpool), Manchester, Leeds, Bradford, Huddersfield, Birmingham, Cambridge, Buckinghamshire and London.

Since 1994 he has taught Economics, Business & Finance, Mathematics, Information Communications Technology, PSHE/Citizenship and also History at various schools in London and Essex.

In 1999 he wrote *Classical Splendour: Roots of Black History* published in the UK by Bogle L'Ouverture Publications. In the same year, he co-authored (with Siaf Millar) *The West African Empire of Songhai,* a textbook used by many schools across the country.

In 2000 he co-authored (again with Siaf Millar) *Sword, Seal and Koran,* another book on the Songhai Empire of West Africa.

In 2006 he wrote the seminal *When We Ruled.* This is still the most advanced synthesis on Ancient and Mediaeval African history ever written by a single author. It was a massive expansion of his earlier book *Classical Splendour: Roots of Black History* and established his reputation as the leading Black History educational service provider.

In 2008 he wrote *Before The Slave Trade,* a highly pictorial companion volume to *When We Ruled.*

Between 2011 and 2014 he wrote a series of e-books for download sold through Amazon Kindle. These e-books covered history, business, religion, music, and science.

In 2013 he co-authored (with Siaf Millar and Saran Keita) *Everyday Life In An Early West African Empire.* It was a massive expansion on the earlier book *Sword, Seal & Koran*. He updated *When We Ruled* by incorporating nearly all of the images from *Before The Slave Trade.* He wrote a trilogy of books entitled *Blacks and Science Volumes One, Two* and *Three.*

In 2014 he wrote *The Rise and Fall of Black Wall $treet and the Seven Key Empowerment Principles, Blacks and Religion Volume One* and *If you want to learn Early African History START HERE.* He also co-authored *African Mathematics: History, Textbook and Classroom Lessons* (with John Matthews).

In 2015 he wrote *19 Lessons in Black History* and *The Black Musical Tradition and Early Black Literature.* He also wrote the book that you are holding right now *Blacks and Religion Volume Two.*

Speaking Engagements

Looking for a speaker for your next event?

The author Robin Walker 'The Black History Man' is dynamic and engaging, both as a speaker and a workshop leader. He brings Black or African history alive, making it relevant for the present generation. You will love his perfect blend of accessibility, engagement, and academic rigour where learning becomes fun.

Walker is available to give speaking engagements to a variety of audiences. He has a highly engaging presentation based on this book. It is called *What did Africa contribute to Judaism, Christianity or Islam?*

To hire Robin Walker for your next event, send an email to historicalwalker@yahoo.com

INDEX

51794717R00089

Made in the USA
Charleston, SC
03 February 2016